D1525049

EIGHTEENTH CENTURY SHAKESPEARE

No. 20

General Editor : Professor Arthur Freeman, Boston University

CURSORY CRITICISMS

O N

Malone's Edition of Shakspeare

Together with

MALONE'S LETTER

T O T H E

Rev. Richard Farmer

CURSORY CRITICISMS

ON

THE EDITION OF

SHAKSPEARE

Published by Edmond Malone.

BY

JOSEPH RITSON

TOGETHER WITH

A LETTER

TO THE

Rev. Richard Farmer, D.D.

Relative to the Edition of Shakspeare,
published in 1790,

And Some Late Criticisms on that Work.

BY

EDMOND MALONE

FRANK CASS & CO. LTD.

1970

96029

Published by
FRANK CASS AND COMPANY LIMITED
67 Great Russell Street, London W.C.1

New Preface Copyright © 1969   Arthur Freeman

Cursory Criticisms

First edition   1792
Reprint of First edition
with a new preface   1970

A Letter to Farmer

First edition   1792
Second edition   1792
Reprint of First edition
with a new preface   1970

ISBN 0 7146 2516 7

Printed in Great Britain by Clarke, Doble & Brendon Ltd.
Plymouth and London

PREFACE

Cursory Criticisms

Among English antiquaries, Joseph Ritson (1752–1803) is held to have been one of the most passionately concerned with minute 'accuracy', as he understood the term, and literal fidelity to old texts in his time. His scholarly disposition as well as his 'wayward and eccentric temper' [*DNB*] led him from extremes of pedantry and self-confident eccentricity (especially orthographic) into vitriolic controversies with such Shakespearean giants as Johnson, Steevens, and Malone, and ultimately, it would appear, to insanity. Nonetheless Ritson's criticism, captious and nit-picking as it may often appear, is as often both correct and useful; it was rarely ignored, if frequently found offensive.

Having flung out twice, in 1783 and 1788, at the edition of Shakespeare prepared by Johnson and Steevens, it might be expected that the great variorum edition (1790) of Edmond Malone, perhaps the crowning glory of eighteenth century Shakespearean scholarship, would draw Ritson's fire as well. It is necessary to distinguish just criticism from prejudice and envy in *Cursory Criticisms*, but more important still to comprehend the difference between Malone's notion of 'restoration'—by collation of 'old copies'—and Ritson's of 'purging the text . . . of all the gross and palpable blunders of the first folio', a labour of taste, 'ear', and 'judgement'—impressionism, we might say, or 'inner light'—as exemplified by the editors he himself commends (p. vii): Rowe, Pope, Theobald, Warburton, and Hanmer—the latter two now considered among the least efficacious Shakespearean scholars of this or any other age. *Cursory Criticisms*, issued anonymously fifteen months after the publication of Malone's *Variorum*, contains its personal slurs on the high-handedness of Malone, its gratuitous patches of anti-Irish quippery, and its overstated extrapolation of relatively meagre evidence; by virtue of the 'errors' exposed Malone is an 'incompetent and unworthy editor', ignorant, blundering, hypercritical (!), guilty of 'international corruption' and 'un-exampled scurrility', '*shallow . . . fond, skill-less, tasteless*', and his work worthy only of 'contempt and derision'; but however caustic and unjust, there is much to be reckoned with in the 'insignificant pamphlet' (Ritson) which mingles its scholarly sense with nearly maniacal invective. It is a curious book, and to be taken, in part, as Malone and all later editors did, quite seriously.

Our text is reprinted from a copy in the possession of the publishers, compared with two copies in the British Museum. It collates [ ]⁴b²A–N⁴, without cancels.

A Letter

Stung by the acerbity as well, perhaps, as the acuity of Ritson's attack on his life work, Malone replied in a published 'Letter' addressed to Richard Farmer, dated 23 April (Shakespeare's supposed birthday, of course), 1792. Malone's choice of Farmer, then fifty-seven, Master of Emmanuel College Cambridge, Librarian of the University, and author of the elegant *Essay on the Learning of Shakespeare* (1767), may have been suggested by Farmer's friendly acquaintance with both parties, although Malone professes no knowledge at all of his antagonist's concealed identity.

Malone defends himself ably and sensibly: among 100,000 lines, more or less, in the text of Shakespeare, containing 1654 new (or *contra*-Steevens) emendations by Malone, Ritson has detected only eight positive mistakes—which Malone 'gladly' accepts and will correct in his forthcoming quarto edition. Five others he disputes. But the main body of Malone's reply concerns itself with the textual authority of the second folio, which he correctly discounts, and which Ritson had traditionally assumed. As such, Malone's *Letter* presents among the earliest persuasive distinctions between authoritative and derivative Elizabethan texts, a re-statement perhaps, but in clearer terms, of arguments its author had offered before and founded his editorial method, to an extent, upon.

Jaggard (p. 206) gives a collation for the first edition of Malone's *Letter* of 'ii.–xl', which corresponds to no copy I have seen, including three I think of the five he locates. All three British Museum examples, including the dedication copy inscribed by Malone to Farmer (642.d.15.[3.]), are paginated with arabic numerals, and collate, as does the present, [ ]²B–C⁸D⁴, with no cancels. A 'second edition', unaltered, was published in the same year. Our text is reprinted from a copy of the first edition in the possession of the publishers.

May 1969   A.F.

CURSORY CRITICISMS

ON THE

EDITION

OF

SHAKSPEARE

PUBLISHED BY

EDMOND MALONE.

A FAULCON, TOW'RING IN HER PRIDE OF PLACE,
WAS BY A MOUSING OWL HAWK'D AT AND KILL'D.

MACBETH.

LONDON:

PRINTED FOR HOOKHAM AND CARPENTER,
NEW AND OLD BOND-STREET.
MDCCXCII.

TO THE

MONTHLY AND CRITICAL

REVIEWERS.

GENTLEMEN,

I PREFIX this addreſs in order
to induce you, before you paſs ſentence on the following pages, to read them through : " *Strike, but
hear !*" To enable you to do this I have deſired my
publiſhers to ſend each of you a copy; for, though
you may have *Jack the Giant-killers coat*, it has
never been ſuſpected that you poſſeſs *Fortunatus's
purſe*; and the title of a book, read in a newſpaper,
or through a ſhop-window, may not be always a ſufficient ground for unqualifyed condemnation and
virulent abuſe.

On ſecond thoughts, however, I believe I might
as well have ſaved them the trouble; ſince you will,
moſt probably, allow Mr. Malone the grateful privilege of reviewing it himſelf: the virtue and honour

of this literary hero frequently condefcending to bring down an unfufpicious enemy from the mafked battery of a Review. And yet, I fee, one of your " gangs"* has the effrontery to boaft that it

——Nothing extenuates,
Nor fets down aught in malice.

That you " nothing extenuate," unlefs it be in favour of yourfelves or your employers, I can eafily believe ; but the next line certainly requires, if not a different reading, an oppofite conftruction. It fuits your purpofe, no doubt, to delude the unwary by falfe colours ; as the devil, when he commences innkeeper, hangs out an angel for his fign. The real meaning, however, is that you

——fet down ALL *in malice.*

Shakfpeares morality, in the hands of a Reviewer, is to be read backward, like a witch's prayer.

* Thefe *focieties of gentlemen* (as they modeftly intitle themfelves) are, with equal juftice and ability, characterifed by Dr. Brown as—" two notorious gangs of *monthly* and *critical* book-thieves, hackney'd in the ways of wickednefs, who, in the rage of hunger and malice, firft *plunder,* and then *abufe, maim,* or *murder,* every honeft author who is poffeffed of ought worth their *carrying off;* yet by fkulking among other vermin in *cellars* and *garrets,* keep their perfons tolerably out of fight, and thus *efcape* the hands of *literary juftice.*" ESTIMATE OF THE MANNERS AND PRINCIPLES OF THE TIMES, vol. II. p. 75.

[v]

Accuftomed as you are to every fpecies of mifreprefentation, you muft by no means do me the injuftice to fay that I treat you with contempt. For,
though a literary proftitute be, in reality, a moft de-
fpicable character, I cannot but confider you in, if
not a far fuperior, at leaft, a very different light ;——
as two formidable, in fhort, and mifchievous gangs
of nocturnal banditti, or invifible footpads, equally
cowardly and malignant, who attack when there can
be no defence, and affaffinate or deftroy where you
cannot plunder. And yet, furprifing as it is, while
offenders of comparative infignificance are almoft
every day expofed on pillories, or perifhing in dun-
geons, you have the luck to efcape the refentment of
the injured, and the vengeance of the law! Upon
my word, gentlemen, I admire your good fortune,
though I cannot perfuade myfelf you deferve it;
and, indeed, as guilt is only hardened by impunity,
the fooner, I think, you are brought to juftice the
better. Nor is this event, perhaps, at fo great a
diftance as you may imagine: even 𝔱𝔥𝔢 𝔐𝔬𝔫𝔰𝔱𝔢𝔯,
you know, was caught at laft ; and, though you poffibly conceive this *brother affaffin* to have been as
inferior to you in cunning, as he certainly was in
criminality, it will not be amifs to let his fate be a
warning to you.

I fhall make no apology for having taken up fo
much of your time, which would, moft probably,
have been worfe employed. You may now pro-

ceed to gratify your malice, and take your revenge ;
and (as I know you are fond of Scripture quotations)
the Lord reward you according to your works!

I am,

Gentlemen,

Your humble fervant,

* *

PREFACE.

MR. MALONE, in the year 1780, when pub-
lishing a *Supplement to Shakspeare* of plays which
he never wrote, modestly remarked that *by a di-*
ligent collation of all the old copies thitherto disco-
vered, and the judicious restoration of ancient readings,
the text of this author seemed then finally settled.
Since that period, however, he has been labouring
" with unceasing solicitude," for the space of " eight
years" to convince the public that he had, if not
directly asserted the thing which was not, at least
gone a little further than was consistent with the
exact state of the case. For, if the text had been
already *diligently collated* with *all the old copies*, why
should he make such a parade of having collated it
himself? If it had not been so collated, why should
he say it had? This fact is therefor manifest, upon
Mr. Malones own evidence, that the text of Shakspeare had never been collated, whether diligently
or not, with all or any of the old copies, by any
person before Mr. Malone. To which one may
add that even this great critics collation has not
been either so diligent or so successful as he would

induce us to believe ;* and alfo that it would have been much better for the faid text if he had never collated it at all. By a *judicious reftoration of ancient readings*, Mr. Malone feems to underftand the re-placing of all the grofs and palpable blunders of the firft folio, from which it has been the labour of fuch

* Of this the following inftances, occafionally noticed, in the *two firft* vols. may ferve as the fpecimen of a proof:

Vol. I. p. 80. " If *thou* be pleas'd"—Both the folios read—*you*.

140. " For love is ftill *more* precious in itfelf."—The old editt. agree in reading—*moft*.

154. " *Speed*. Item, fhe can *few*.

" *Launce*. That's as much as to fay, can fhe *fo*."
Both the folios read *fow*, which is manifeftly requifite. Probably, however, the editor may fuppofe *few* and *fo* to have the fame pronunciation.

155. " And that *I cannot* help." In the old editions —*cannot I*.

174. " As eafily as I do tear *this* paper." Both folios read—*his*.

Vol. II. p. 70. " But grace being the foul of your complexion *fhould* keep the body of it ever fair."—In the folios—*fhall*.

71. " Let me hear you fpeak *further*." Both edi-tions—*farther*; a word entirely different from *further*, though too frequently confounded with it by ignorant perfons : the one being the com-parative of *forth*; the other a corruption of *farer*.

143. " In what fafe place you have *difpos'd* my mo-ney." The old editions read—*beftow'd*

151. " If it be, fir, *pray* eat none of it." In the folio —*I pray*.

157. " Ay let none enter"—The old copies —Ay, *and* let.

critics as **Rowe**, Pope, Theobald, Warburton, and Hanmer to purge the text. Mr. Malone is a critic of a very different defcription.

I have thought proper, in the following pages, to make a few obfervations on fome of Mr. Malones notes. Now Mr. Malone will take this exceedingly ill; for Mr. Malone has a very high opinion of himfelf, and a very mean one of every body elfe. But I confefs I do not feek to pleafe Mr. Malone: I wifh to refcue the language and fenfe of an admirable author from the barbarifm and corruption they have acquired in paffing through the hands of this incompetent and unworthy editor. In a word, I mean to convi&t and not to convince him.

The total want of *ear* and *judgement*, under which Mr. Malone will be found to labour, is undoubtedly a natural defe&t, for which he would be an

---

Vol. II. p. 190. "And much different from the man he was." The folios read : " And much *much* different ;" —the additional fyllable being neceffary to the metre, which the editor could not perceive.

Ibi. " And *therefore* came it that the man was mad." In the old copies.—" And *thereof* came it."

477. " Through the foreft have I gone, " But Atherian *found* I none." All the old editions read—*find*, which is not only more elegant but more grammatical.

There is no reafon to believe that each of the remaining volumes would not have contributed an equal number of thefe damning proofs; but in fa&t the fearch required too large a portion of both time and patience.

object rather of pity than of reprehenfion, if he had not forced himfelf into an employment for which ear and judgement were effential, and nature, of courfe, in depriving him of thofe indifpenfable requifites, had utterly difqualifyed him. Want of courage, in a common man, may be confidered as mere weaknefs of nerves; in a commander, it is punifhed with death.

But it is not the want of ear and judgement only of which I have to accufe Mr. Malone: he ftands charged with divers other high crimes and mifdemeanors againft the divine majefty of our fovereign lord of the drama; with deforming his text, and degrading his margin, by intentional corruption, flagrant mifreprefentation, malignant hypercriticifm, and unexampled fcurrility. Thefe charges fhall be proved—not, as Mr. Malone proves things, by groundlefs opinion and confident affertion, but—by fact, argument, and demonftration. How fayeft thou, culprit? Guilty or not guilty?

Whoever may think fit to cenfure the language of thefe " criticifms," Mr. Malone has no fuch right; having himfelf rifled the blooming beds of Billingsgate to grace·his commentaries with the choiceft rhetorical flowers.* It is furely lawful to return an

* He feldom introduces the author of the *Remarks*, &c. without a compliment on his *profound ignorance* or *crude notions*, the *feeblenefs of his attempts at jocularity*, the *flendernefs of his criticifm*, and the like; or the favourite epithet of *a fhallow* or *half-informed remarker*. " And thus the whirligig of time brings in his revenges."

enemy the fhot of his own poifoned arrows : and, as
for the reft, whatever refpect may be due to the
errors of genius, the blunders of ignorance and pre-
fumption deferve no quarter.

*** Since thefe fheets were printed off, Mr.
Malone has iffued propofals for a new and fplendid
edition of the plays and poems of this admired
author, IN FIFTEEN VOLUMES ROYAL
QUARTO ! ! ! The reciprocal good opinion which
the public and Mr. Malone appear to entertain of
each other does both parties infinite honour ; the
one from his fingular confidence, the other from its
refined tafte.   Having fufficiently, and, I truft, fatis-
factorily, proved how peculiarly qualifyed this ingenious gentleman is for an editor of our great poet,
I have only to add my fincereft wifhes that the com-
pletion of fo magnificent a work may happen in
time to afford me another equally favorable opportunity of giving my humble teftimony to his very
extraordinary merit.

   O ! while, along the ftream of time, thy name
Expanded flies, and gathers all its fame,
Say, fhall my little bark attendant fail,
Purfue the triumph, and partake the gale ?

CURSORY CRITICISMS, &c.

VOL. I. PART I.

PREFACE.

PP. xix. xxi. &c.

THERE cannot well be a more flagrant proof of disingenuity in the support of a particular opinion than is here manifested by the editor in his treatment of the *second folio*, in order to substantiate his position " that the editor of that book was intirely ignorant of our poets phraseology and metre ; and that various alterations were made by him, in consequence of that ignorance, which render his edition of no value whatever." Many of the instances adduced in support of this assertion are mere self-evident errors of the press, the accidental omission or insertion of a single word, or the inadvertent transposition of a couple of letters ; * faults to which every copy is

---

* One passage of this kind is very remarkable. The first folio reading.

     Is ftraightway *calm* and boarded with a pirate

The editor of the second edition, or some one for him, had added the *d* ; and the printer made it *claim'd*. So where, instead of *Carrat*, in the first folio, the second has *Raccat* ; and instead of *vigilance*, *viligance*, we are to impute the compositors carelesness to ignorance or intentional corruption.

A

equally fubject; and confequently prove that editors
ignorance much lefs than his accufers malice; which
is the more remarkable as he has actually availed
himfelf of a very confiderable number of the corrections of the identical edition which he thus anxi-
oufly labours to depreciate as a fink of ignorance and
corruption. It muft be evident, that by this partial mode of proceeding, the fame charge might be
brought home not only to the firft folio, but to almoft
any edition of any author. A perfon who had
only truth and juftice in view would have exhibited
a faithful ftatement, a fair debtor and creditor account of the merits and defects of the two editions.
But this method, Mr. Malone is confcious, fo far
from anfwering his purpofe, would have completely
difproved and given the *lye direct* to his accufation;
fince, in fact, for *one* inftance of an alteration for
the worfe it will be eafy to produce *ten* inftances of
alterations for the better, and fuch, at the fame time,
as not only no ignorant or capricious perfon, but
not even a man of fenfe and fagacity would have hit
upon, without the affiftance. of manufcript corrections or perfonal information: and after all, it is
not in the leaft improbable that both editions were
printed by one and the fame perfon, there being
only *nine* years difference in their dates, and the
one, whether intentionally or otherwife, juft as in-
accurate as the other. Both editors, at leaft, if two
there were, were Shakfpeares contemporaries; pro-

bably his acquaintance ; poffibly his friends ; and, in all events, equally familiar with the language of his time and his peculiar phrafeology. But, leaving Mr. Malones partiality and ingratitude out of the queftion, I am by no means difpofed to admit his judgement as to any ones ignorance of Shakfpeares phrafeology and metre ; in neither of which, I believe, we fhall find him a proficient. Some of thefe identical in-ftances prove the direct reverfe of what they are brought to do, and convict the profecutor of both ignorance and malignity.

I. " His [*i. e.* the fecond editors] ignorance of Shakfpeares phrafeology" confifts in printing—

" I can go *no* further," inftead of " I can *not* go *no* further ;"

" *I* appointed him," inftead of " *I am* appointed him ;" the fyllable having flipped out in the prefs :

" The way to *ftudy* death," inftead of " the way to *dufty* death ;" a mere accidental tranfpofition of two letters ; which is conftantly happening. The following is of more confequence.

" The feventh [fifth] fcene of the fourth act of this play [*Antony and Cleopatra*] concludes with thefe words :—" Difpatch,—Enobarbus !" Anthony, who, is the fpeaker, defires his attendant *Eros* to difpatch, and then pronounces the name *Enobarbus,* who had recently deferted him, and whofe lofs he here la-ments. But there being no perfon in the fcene but Eros, and the point being inadvertently omitted after the word *difpatch*, the editor of the fecond folio fuppofed that Enobarbus muft have been an error of the prefs, and therefore reads ;

" Difpatch, *Eros.*"

Such is Mr. Malones account of the matter, in which it is only neceffary to fupply a fmall omiffion of the very accurate writer, *viz.* that the line, of which the two words in queftion are part, is intended for metre, of which he is too good a judge for the omiffion to have been defigned. This intention, however, would be defeated by the word *Enobarbus* ; unlefs we are to accent it thus :

—my fortunes have
Corrupted honeft men. Difpatch.—*Enōbărbŭs ?*

Antony is continually repeating the name of Eros ; he does it no lefs than five times in the preceding fcene, and once before in this. The manufcript, it is probable, had, in this place, only an *E.* of which the original printer improperly made *Enobarbus :* this miftake muft have been fome how or other made known to the editor of the fecond folio, moft likely by a MS. correction in the copy he printed from ; he has therefor rightly corrected the word, but, at the fame time, has neglected to obferve the tranfpofition which had been made by his predeceffor (fuppofing the printer of each copy two different perfons). Take the line, therefor, as Shakfpeare gave it, and let us acknowlege our obligation to the fecond folio, for fo valuable an alteration :

Corrupted honeft men.—*Eros ! difpatch.*

If he had meant that Anthony fhould apoftrophife his abfent officer, he would have given it thus :

Corrupted honeft men.—*O Enobarbus !*

The editor of the fecond folio was therefor right in fuppofing, if indeed he was not fure, " that Eno-barbus muft have been an error of the prefs."

" In *K. Henry VIII.* are thefe lines

" —If we did think
" His *contemplation* were above the earth,—"

Not underftanding this phrafeology, and fuppofing that *were* muft require a noun in the plural number, he reads :

" —If we did think
" His *contemplations* were above the earth, &c."

Now, one would be glad to know where there is a fingle perfon to be found, fetting afide this petulant dogmatift, who ever heard of fuch a phrafeology, or who does not know " that *were* muft require a noun in the plural number."

It would be well if charges of no better founda-tion or greater ftrength could be brought againft the ignorance of M. Malone.

II. " Let us now examine how far he was acquainted with the *metre* of thefe plays." Ay marry,
now for it; this is a fubjeƈt upon which we are
quite at home.

> " In the *Winter's Tale*, we find,—
> " What wheels ? racks ? fires ? what flaying ?
> boiling ?
> " In leads, or oils ?":—

" Not knowing that *fires* was ufed as a diffyllable
he added the word *burning* at the end of the line."

He did fo; and it will be evident to every one
who can read that the addition was abfolutely neceffary, in point of quantity, to the perfeƈtion of the
line.   Mr. Malone can *not* read, and is totally ignorant of the confequences of his own abfurd ideas;
he could never elfe have thought fuch a line as the
following confiftent with the laws of metre:

> " What wheels ? racks ? *fi-ers ?* what *flay-
> ing ? boiling ?*

Thus, however, he infifts that Shakfpeare intended
us to read—*fwor-en*, *cha-rums*, inftead of *fworn*,
tharms; *fu-ar*, for *fure*, &c. &c. converting one
fyllable into two, two into three or four and fo on.

Inftead of

> " And fo to *arms*, viƈtorious *noble* father,"

with the *fecond* folio, we are to read

" And fo to *a-rums, vic-to-ri-ous* father,"

becaufe *noble,* or fome other word of equal quantity, has been omited by the printer of the *firft.*

Inftead of

" *But* prove it, *Henry,* and thou fhalt be king."

As given by the editor of the fecond folio, " not knowing Henry to be ufed as a trifyllable," we are to read :

" Prove it, *He-nē-ry,* and thou fhalt be king."

Inftead of

" Pours into captains wounds ! *ha!* banifh-
    ment.

pours being a diffyllable, we are to adopt the follow-ing harmonious line :

" *Po-ūrs* in-*tō cap-tāins* wounds ! banifhment.

Inftead of

She's tickled now, her fume *can* need no fpurs.

he thinks it more in the authors manner to read :

" She's *tickeléd* now ; *hér* fume needs no
    fpurs,"

Inftead of

" The body of *the* city, country, court :"
" The body of *ci-tỳ, coun-tē-ry,* court."

And inftead of

" *Burn* hotter than my faith.   O but *dear* fir.
" *Bu-ūrn hot-tēr* than *mȳ* faith.   O but fir."

" The editor, indeed" he fays, " was even ignorant of the author's manner of accenting words, for
in the *Tempeſt*, where we find,

" —Spirits, which by mine art
" I have from their *confines* call'd to enact
" My prefent fancies,"—

he exhibits the fecond line thus :

" I have from *all* their *confines* call'd to enact."

It is fomewhat lucky, however, for the editor of the
fecond folio, that we are able to produce in his defence no lefs decifive a teftimony than that of Shakfpeare himfelf.   The word in queftion occurs in
Julius Cæfar :

" And Cæfar's fpirit, ranging for revenge,
" Shall, on thefe *cònfines*, with a monarch's voice,
" Cry havock, and let flip the dogs of war."

The reader will now judge for himfelf which of
thefe two editors, the profecutor or defendant, is
moft ignorant of his authors " phrafeology, metre,"
and " manner of accenting words."

" Had he confulted the original quarto," fays
Mr. Malone, " he would have found that the poet

wrote"—fo and fo. Well, but how if he could not get, or never heard of the original quarto? how then? Had he not, in common with every other editor, the right of fupplying imperfections or correcting miftakes, according to the beft of his judgement? It is no imputation upon the fagacity of Dr. Thirlby or fir Thomas Hammer that they have fuggefted readings, which, however plaufible, are difproved by the more recent difcovery of the old quartos : all of which have not been yet feen, even by Mr. Malone ; who has, at the fame time, been indebted to chance or favour for many of the others ; for which he has not, on every occafion, made the moft grateful or liberal return.

I fhall now proceed to make the editor of the fecond folio fome amends for the injuftice, malevolence, and perfonal abufe of his Hibernian adverfary, by difplaying a few inftances not only of his actual fuperiority to his predeceffor (if, in fact, either edition had any other editor than the compofitor of the prefs), but alfo where that fuperiority is admitted by Mr. Malones own adoption. The latter cafe is diftinguifhed by an afterifk. It was once my intention to have given, what Mr. Malone ought to have done, a fair and faithful collation of the various readings of the two editions ; but the fpace and prefs-work required even by the following fpecimen and the neceffity I fhould have thought myfelf under of going through them a fecond time, which no one

needs to be told is a work of time and patience, will
be a fufficient apology for not having carryed it into
effect at prefent. However, as Mr. Malone has
preferved all the *errors* of the fecond folio, and I
fhall exhibit a confiderable number, at leaft, of its
emendations, the reader will, between us, have a tolerably complete view of the controverfy. The firft
reading is that of the folio 1623, the other that of
the folio 1632.

TEMPEST.

I'll fhew thee every fertile inch o'th' *ifland*.
I'l fhew thee every fertile inch o'th' *ile*.

————*who* t'advance and *who*
To trafh for overtopping.
————*whom* t'advance, and *whom*
To trafh for overtopping.

If I fhould fay I faw fuch *iflands*.
If I fhould fay I faw fuch *iflanders*.*

Earths increafe, foifon plenty.
Earths increafe, *and* foifon plenty.

You brother mine that *entertaine* ambition.
You brother mine that *entertain'd* ambition.

TWO GENTLEMEN OF VERONA.

You conclude then that my mafter is a fhepherd, and
I fheep.

You conclude then that my mafter is a fhepherd,
and I *a* fheep.*

You have *ceftern'd* me.
You have *teftern'd* me.*

I fee you have a *months* mind to them.
I fee you have a *monthes* mind to them.

With *Valentinus* in the emperors court.
With *Valentino* in the emperors court.

If thou wilt go to the alehoufe.
If thou wilt go to the alehoufe, *fo.* *

And inftances *of* infinite of love.
And inftances *as* infinite of love.*

That they fhould harbour where their lord *fhould* be.
That they fhould harbour where their lord *would* be.

Who would'ft thou ftrike.
Whom would'ft thou ftrike.*

Who Silvia ?
Whom Silvia ? *

Therefore know *thee* for this I entertain thee.
Therefore know *thou* for this I entertain thee.*

It feems you lov'd not her *not* leave her token.
It feems you lov'd not her *to* leave her token.

Which of you faw Eglamour of late.
Which of you faw *fir* Eglamour of late. *

For fuch is a friend now, treacherous man.
For fuch is a friend now *thou* treacherous man.

MERRY WIVES OF WINDSOR.

Hold firrah, bear thefe letters *tightly*.
Hold firrah, bear thefe letters *rightly*. †

We cannot mifufe enough.
We cannot mifufe *him* enough. *

Let him ftrike the old woman.
Let him *not* ftrike the old woman. *

MEASURE FOR MEASURE.

Where youth and coft witlefs bravery keeps.
Where youth and coft *and* witlefs bravery keeps. *

More reafons *in* this action.
More reafons *for* this action.

May call it again.   Well believe this.
May call it *back* again.   Well, believe this.

† Thus alfo the old quarto. *Tightly*, however, being ftark nonfenfe, is judicioufly preferred by Mr. Malone.

Than the foft myrtle, but man proud man.
Than the foft myrtle, *O* but man, proud man. †

Bring them to fpeak where I may be conceal'd.
Bring them to fpeak where I may be conceal'd.
  Yet near them.

The *prenzie* Angelo.
The *princely* Angelo.*

In *prenzie* guards.
In *princely* guards.*

That age ache *periurie* and imprifonment.
That age ache *penurie* and imprifonment.*

Was affianced to her oath.
Was affianced to her *by* oath.*

From our faults as faults from feeming free.
Free from our faults, as faults from feeming free.

Firft let her fhew *your* face.
Firft let her fhew *her* face.*

Although by *confutation* they are ours.
Although by *confifcation* they are ours.* ‡

---

† This, fays Malone, " like *all the other emendations* of that copy,
is the *worft* and *moft improbable* that could have been chofen." *Ipfe
dixit !* He propofes—" but man, *weak,* proud man."

‡ *Confutation,* however, he thinks, " may be right, by his being
confuted." If that is the cafe Mr. Malone himfelf may be right.

(14)

COMEDY OF ERRORS.

And by me had not our hap been bad.
And by me *too* had not our hap been bad.＊

A mean woman was delivered.
A *poor* mean woman was delivered.＊

Which being violently born *up*.
Which being violently born *upon*.＊

Gave *healthful* welcome to their fhipwreck'd guefts.
Gave *helpful* welcome to their fhipwreck'd guefts.＊

What *have* befall'n of them and *they* till now.
What *hath* befall'n of them and *thee* till now.＊

That his attendant *(fo* his cafe was like).
That his attendant *(for* his cafe was like).＊

Look when I ferve him fo he takes it.
Look when I ferve him fo he takes it *ill.* †

Would that *a love* he would detain.
Would that *alone* he would detain.＊

Here is no time for all things.
There is no time for all things.＊

In no time to recover hair loft by nature.
No time to recover hair loft by nature.＊

† This word, he fays, which the rime *feems to countenance,* was
furnifhed, &c. Q. If the rime does not abfolutely require it, ₒr
he can find another to fupply its place.

We talk with goblins owls and fprites.
We talk with goblins owls and *elves* [elvifh] fprites.*

I'll meet you at that place fome hour hence.
I'll meet you at that place fome hour *fir* hence.

Ill deeds *is* doubled with an evil word.
Ill deeds *are* doubled with an evil word.

To drown me in thy *fifter* flood of tears.
To drown me in thy *fifters* flood of tears.

And as a *bud* I'll take thee and there lie.
And as a *bed* I'll take thee and there lie. *

Making war againft her *heir*.
Making war againft her *hair*. *

And then, fir, fhe bears away our fraughtage, fir.
Then, fir, fhe bears away our fraughtage, fir.

Oh his hearts meteors tilting in his face.
Of his hearts meteors tilting in his face.

Thus he, unknown to me, fhould be in debt.
That he unknown to me fhould be in debt.

Mafter, if do, expect fpoon meat.
Mafter, if *you* do, expect fpoon meat. *

LOVES LABOUR LOST.

Well fitted in arts, glorious in arms.
Well fitted in *the* arts, glorious in arms. *

Well, I will love, write, sigh, pray, sue, groan.
Well, I will love, write, sigh, pray, sue *and* groan.

The *prayful* princess—
The *praiseful* princess. *

With men like men, of inconstancy.
With men like men, of *strange* inconstancy.

It mourns that painting usurping hair.
It mourns that painting *and* usurping hair.

And shape his service wholly to my *device*.
And shape his service wholly to my *behefts*. * †

As gravitys revolt to *wantons be*.
As gravitys revolt to *wantonness*. *

But, while 'tis spoke, each turn away *his* face.
But while 'tis spoke each turn away *her* face. *

The rest will *e'er* come in if he be out.
The rest will *ne'er* come in if he be out.

They were all in lamentable cases.
O they were all in lamentable cases.

This jest is dry to me.—Gentle sweet.
This jest is dry to me.—*fair*, gentle sweet.

† " One of the very few corrections of any value to be found in that copy." MALONE.

MIDSUMMER NIGHTS DREAM.

This *man* hath bewitched the bofom of my child.
This hath bewitch'd the bofom of my child.*

Unto his lordfhip whofe unwifh'd yoke.
Unto his lordfhip *to* whofe unwifh'd yoke.

For I am fick when I do look on *you*.
For I am fick when I do look on *thee*.*

Tranfparent Helena, Nature fhews art.
Tranfparent Helena, Nature *here* fhews art.

MERCHANT OF VENICE.

If a Chriftian *do* not play the knave and get thee.
If a Chriftian *did* not play the knave and get thee.*

So begone, you are fped.
So begone *fir*, you are fped.

There is no *voice* fo fimple.
There is no *vice* fo fimple.*

More rich than *onely to* ftand high in your account.
More rich than *to* ftand high in your account.

And ne'er a true one.   In fuch a night.
And ne'er a true one.   *And* in fuch a night.

AS YOU LIKE IT.

After my flight.   Now *go in we* content.
After my flight.   Now *go we in* content.*

C

To that which had too *muſt*.
To that which had too *much*.*

Know you not maſter to *ſeeme* kind of men
Know you not maſter to *ſome* kind of men.*

Wearing thy hearer in thy miſtreſs praiſe
Wearying thy hearer in thy miſtreſs praiſe.*

——ſearching of they *would*.
——ſearching of they [thy] *wound*.*

And I remember the kiſſing of her *batler*.
And I remember the kiſſing of her *batlet*.

Good even to *your* friend.
Good even to *you* friend.*

Thou art right welcome as thy *maſters* is.
Thou art right welcome as thy *maſter* is.*

Have more cauſe to hate him than to love him.
I have more cauſe, &c.

Let me better acquainted with thee.
Let me *be* better acquainted with thee.*

In which *by* often rumination.
In which *my* often rumination.*

Like a ripe ſiſter : the woman low.
Like a ripe ſiſter : *but* the woman low.

My gentle Phebe *did* bid me give you this. †
My gentle Phebe bid me give you this.

† So Malone. *Phebe* muſt therefor be a monoſyllable.

TAMING OF THE SHREW.

Were fhe *is* as rough.
Were fhe as rough.*

Of all thy fuitors here I charge tell.
Of all thy fuitors here I charge *thee* tell.*

No fuch fir, as you, if me you mean.
No fuch *jade* fir, as you, if me you mean.*

Much more a fhrew of impatient humour.
Much more a fhrew of *thy* impatient humour.*

As before imparted to your worfhip.
As *I* before imparted to your worfhip.*

As much news as *wilt thou.*
As much news as *thou wilt.**

I fear it is too *cholerick* a meat.
I fear it is too *phlegmatick* a meat. †

Then at my lodging, an it like you.
Then at my lodging, an it like you, *fir.*

I cannot tell, *expect* they are bufied in a counterfeit
  affurance.
I cannot tell, *except* they are bufied in a counterfeit
  affurance.

---

† It is a *neats foot*, which cannot be thought to engender *choler*.
Befides, the word *cholerick*, which Malone prefers, occurs three lines
lower.

He will make the man mad to make *the* woman
of him.

He will make the man mad to make *a* woman of
him.*

Whither away or *whither* is thy abode.
Whither away or *where* is thy abode.*

Didſt thou never ſee thy *miſtreſs* father ?
Didſt thou never ſee thy *maſters* father ?*

Well, I ſay no : and therefore, *ſir*, aſſurance.
Well, I ſay no : and therefore *for* aſſurance.*

ALL'S WELL THAT ENDS WELL.

It blots thy beauty as froſts *do* bite the meads.
It blots thy beauty as froſts bite the meads.*

Yet in this captious and *intemible* ſieve.
Yet in this captious and *intenible* ſieve.*

And would not have knaves thrive long under.
And would not have knaves thrive long under *her*.*

TWELFTH NIGHT.

Yet you will be hang'd *to* be turn'd away.
Yet you will be hang'd, *or* be turned away.

Enter Violenta.
Enter Viola.

That methought her eyes had loſt her tongue.
That *ſure* methought her eyes had loſt her tongue.*

Let thy tongue *langer* with arguments of ftate.
Let thy tongue *tang* with arguments of ftate.*

—clear *ftores.*
—clear *ftones.*

With hey, the thrufh and the jay.
With hey, *with hey,* the thrufh and the jay.*

Digeft with a cuftom.
Digeft *it* with a cuftom.

Burn hotter than my faith.   O but fir.
Burn hotter than my faith.   O but *dear* fir.

Before this ancient fir, *whom,* it fhould feem.
Before this ancient fir, *who,* it fhould feem.*

Of excellent witchcraft, *whom* perforce muft know.
Of excellent witchcraft, *who,* perforce muft know.*

You know *my* fathers temper.
You know *your* fathers temper.*

With her *who* here I cannot hold on fhore.
With her *whom* here I cannot hold on fhore.*

Of kernes and gallow-*groffes*—
Of kernes and gallow-*glaffes*—

Shipwrecking ftorms and direful thunders.
Shipwrecking ftorms and direful thunders *breaking*
  [break].

Is execution done on Cawdor *or* not
Thofe in commiffion yet return'd?
Is execution done on Cawdor? *Are* not
Thofe in commiffion yet return'd.*

Whom we to gain our *peace* have fent to peace.
Whom we to gain our *place* have fent to peace.*

Whether, in deed, before *they* here approach.
Whether, indeed, before *thy* here-approach.

K. JOHN.

It would not be fir Nob in any cafe.
I would not be fir Nob in any cafe.

Say, fhall the current of our right *roam* on.
Say fhall the current of our right *run* on.*

Strong reafons make *ftrange* actions.
Strong reafons make *ftrong* actions. †

'Tis true to hurt his mafter, no *mans* elfe.
'Tis true to hurt his mafter, no *man* elfe.*

† Malone, in this, as in other places, prefers the *nonfenfe* of the
firft edition to the *fenfe* of the fecond.

FIRST PART OF K. HENRY IV.

With fuch a heady *currance.*
With fuch a heady *current.**

To furnifh with all appertinents.
To furnifh *him* with all appertinents.*

Which in fufferance heartily will rejoice.
Which *I* in fufferance heartily will rejoice.*

To his full height.   On, on, you *noblifh* Englifh.
To his full height.   On, on, you *noblest* Englith.*

Of *headly* murder.
Of *heady* murder.*

Poor we call them in their native lords.
Poor we *may* call them in their native lords.

Pales in the flood with men, wives, and boys.
Pales in the flood with men, *with* wives and boys.*

FIRST PART OF K. HEN. VI.

Shall be *whipt* out in the next parliament.
Shall be *wip'd* out in the next parliament.*

If Richard will be true, not that *all alone.*
If Richard will be true, not that *alone.*

Yes, my lord, her father is a king.
Yes, my *good* lord, her father is a king.*

She's tickled now, her fume *needs* no spurs.
She's tickled now, her fume *can need* no spurs.

Truft nobody, for fear you betray'd.
Truft nobody for fear you *be* betray'd.*

When I return with victory *to* the field.
When I return with victory *from* the field.*

To Lynn, my lord; and *fhip* from thence to Flanders.
To Lynn, my lord; and *fhipt* from thence to Flanders.

HENRY VIII.

Good man, thofe joyful tears fhew thy true *hearts*.
Good man, thofe joyful tears fhew thy true *heart*.

JULIUS CÆSAR.

Are then in council, and the ftate of *a* man.
Are then in council, and the ftate of man.

Paffion I fee is catching *from* mine eyes.
Paffion I fee is catching, *for* mine eyes.

For I have neither *writ*, nor words nor worth.
For I have neither *wit*, nor words nor worth.

CORIOLANUS.

Our beft friends made, our means ftretch'd.
Our beft friends made, *and* our *beft* means ftretch'd *out*.

ANTHONY AND CLEOPATRA.

—my fortunes have
Corrupted honeſt men. Diſpatch *Enobarbus.*
—my fortunes have
Corrupted honeſt men. Diſpatch *Eros.* [Eros, diſpatch !]

Let him come in. *What a poor* inſtrument.
Let him come in. *How poor an* inſtrument.

TITUS ANDRONICUS.

Was none in Rome to make a ſtale.
Was *there* none *elſe* in Rome to make a ſtale *of*.*

Even from *Eptons* riſing in the eaſt.
Even from *Hyperions* riſing in the eaſt.*

ROMEO AND JULIET.

Jul. Romeo !
Rom. My *niece.*
Jul. Romeo !
Rom. My *ſweet.*

Misſhapen chaos of *well-ſeeing* forms.
Misſhapen chaos of well-*ſeeming* forms.

Among freſh *fennell* buds—
Among freſh *female* buds—

A *dimne* ſaint, an honorable villain.
A *damned* ſaint, an honorable villain.

D

(26)

But *which* a rear-ward following Tybalts death.
But *with* a rear-ward following Tybalts death.

The rofes in thy lips and cheeks fhall fade
To *many* afhes——
The rofes in thy lips and cheeks fhall fade
To *mealy* afhes——

HAMLET.

——*this* purfy times.
——*thefe* purfy times.*

Lord Hamlet is a prince out of thy *Starre.*
Lord Hamlet is a prince out of thy *fphere.*

The *inobled* queen.
The *mobled* queen.

OTHELLO.

Out ran my purpofe ; and I return'd *then* rather
Out ran my purpofe and I return'd *the* rather——*

Did Michael Caffio, when you woo'd my lady
Know of your love ?
I did not think he had been acquainted with *her.*
Did &c.
Know &c.
I did not think he had been acquainted with *it.*

P. 249.

" The Quip Modeſt, &c."

☞ " THE author of this pamphlet, after a few copies had got abroad, had the *modeſty* to ſuppreſs it. Some time afterwards, repenting as it were of his repentance, he iſſued it out. One inſtance may be ſufficient to ſhew his *profound ignorance* of the poet whom he attempted to illuſtrate ; he ſuppoſed the words *ignomy* and *intergatory*, in a late edition of Shakſpeare, to be errours of the preſs ! So, when the clown in *Meaſure for Meaſure* ſays " there were but two ſtew'd prunes in the houſe, which at that very *diſtant* time ſtood, as it were in a fruit-diſh, &c. this Remarker for *diſtant* would read *inſtant*."

The veracity of this note is no leſs remarkable than its decency. That the author of the pamphlet in queſtion ever " had the modeſty to ſuppreſs it" is an abſolute falſehood, known to his printer, his bookſeller, and all who bought it. The truth is that, " after a few copies were got abroad," the further ſale was delayed till a leaf could be reprinted, in which ſome erroneous references had been detected, and an expreſſion uſed which was thought too ſtrong for the perſon alluded to, even if that perſon had been Mr. Malone, and another added to convict the

editor or revifer of the " late edition" of a grofs and
wilful mifreprefentation. All this might take up a
week, when the publication was continued. As to
the reft, both Mr. Malone and the author of that
pamphlet may have fufficient reafon to wifh that
neither of them had ever betrayed more *profound ignorance* of this great poet than in barely prefering
the reading of one edition to that of another. That
ignominy, the correction of the fecond folio, and of
which *ignomy* is every where either a contraction or
a corruption, is requifite in the prefent inftance will
be evident to all, except Mr. Malone, and perhaps
the editor (or revifer) of the edition in queftion,
from the line itfelf:

" *Ignòminy* in ranfom and free pardon."

Intergatories, is likewife nothing more than a
contraction of *interrogatories*, as Shakfpeare would
always have written it, if his metre had not required
the facrifice of a fyllable, which profe does not. So,
in *K. John :*

" What earthly name to *interrògatories*."

Inftant is alfo the reading of the fecond folio, and
of every other edition before that of 1785. As
however it was thought *diftant* might be intentional,
the inftance was omitted in the cancel.

After all, if the " *Quipfters ignorance*" of his
author was fo " *profound*," why has this infallible

judge adopted any of his remarks or fuggeftions, fometimes word for word, and elfewhere with *fneaking approbation*, or at fecond-hand. See vol. ii. 11. 256. 491. 507. iii. 27. 77. 316. 394. iv. 497. 504. vi. 146. 273. v. 459. viii. 634. &c. &c. How fay you to this M. Malone?

VOL. I. PART II.

P. 293.

" *Richard the Confeffor.*"

" THIS piece," Mr. Malone obferves, " fhould feem to have been written by the tinker in *The Taming of the Shrew*, who talks of *Richard Conqueror*." Unfortunately, however, the obfervation is but one out of many inftances of our " half-informed" editors pleafantry being occafioned by his ignorance. He fuppofes *Richard* a blunder for *Edward*; becaufe he does not know that there is fuch a perfonage as *Richard the Confeffor*; whereas there are no lefs than *four Confeffors of that name*, any of whom might have been, and one certainly was, the hero of the above play. In the firft place there is faint *Richard the Confeffor*, an imaginary king of England, fuppofed to be buried at Lucca, where he is faid to have dyed on his return from a pilgrimage to Rome. Another was bifhop of Chichefter; a

third of St. Andrews in Calabria; and the fourth
hermit of Hampole near Doncaster, whose somni-
ferous lucubrations have contributed in no small degree to the bulk of Mr. Wartons *History of English
Poetry*. All of these are exprefsly ftiled *Confefsors*
in the *English Martyrologe*, 1608, and other books
of the fame caft: fo that the editors " attempt at
jocularity" is as " feeble" as his " ignorance" is
" profound."

TEMPEST.

P. 21.

Pro. Go make thyfelf like a nymph o'the fea;
    be fubject
To no fight but thine and mine; invifible
To every eye-ball elfe.

The elder folio regulates the paffage thus:

Go make thyfelf like a nymph o'th' fea:
Be fubject to no fight but thine and mine; invifible
To every eye-ball elfe.

The fecond reads:

——like *to* a nymph o'th' fea.

And now comes our Irifh editor, and pronounces
as pofitively as if he had been at the copyifts or
compofitors elbow that the words *be fubject* were
transfered to the fecond line " by the carelefsnefs of

the tranfcriber or printer." " The regulation that
I have made," fays he, " fhews that the addition [of
the fecond folio] was unneceffary."

The only difference between the editor of the
fecond folio and Mr. Malone is that the former per-
fected the metre of the only defective line, and the
latter has deftroyed that of each. Had this " very
fond and fkill-lefs" editor poffeffed one thoufandth
part of the fenfe and fagacity he affumes the credit
of, he would have perceived that the blunder of the
tranfcriber or printer confifted, not in tranfpofing the
words *be fubject*, but, in the infertion of two other
fyllables which certainly have no bufinefs there, and
could not poffibly have come from Shakfpeare,
unlefs Shakfpeare had written like Mr. Malone.
" The regulation that *I* have made fhews that the
addition was neceffary :" I appeal to thofe who have
ears :

> Go make thyfelf like to a nymph o'th' fea,
> Be fubject to no fight but mine, invifible
> To every eye-ball elfe.

If this alteration have been made already, it is
more than I know.

P. 24.

" Curf'd be I that I did fo !—all the *charms*."

" The latter word *(charms)*" we are told " like
many others of the fame kind is here ufed as a diffyllable."

How other words " of the fame kind" may be used is of little confequence : all we want to know is why the word *charms* fhould be fo ufed; or, in fhort, how one fyllable comes to be two. The metre of the line is manifeftly and fimply perfect, as confifting of ten monofyllables, alternately fhort and long : fo that it is abfolutely impoffible to conceive a lefs exceptionable inftance of heroic verfe. Is this laborious octennial editor ignorant that his authors meafure confifts of *ten fyllables ?* or is he, like many of his wild countrymen, unable to reckon to ten, or to count his fingers? The only reafon, I can perceive, for his making *charms* a word of two fyllables, is that it cannot poffibly be more than one.

P. 37.

—the fair foul herfelf
Weigh'd, between lothnefs and obedience, at
Which end *o'the* beam *fhe'd* bow.

The old edition reads—*fhould*—and Mr. Pope, by the omiffion of a fingle fuperfluous letter—

Which end *the* beam *fhould* bow ;

an eafy and appofite fenfe, which our ingenious and confiftent critic, who thinks that " an omiffion of any word in the old copy," however nonfenfical or abfurd, " without fubftituting another in its place, is *feldom fafe*," has rejected for a much more violent alteration, and no fenfe at all.

P. 39.

" Bourn, bound of land, tilth, vineyard, none.

" *Bourn,*" the editor fays, " might have been ufed as a *diſſyllable.*"

Certainly,—by fuch a judge of harmony as himſelf.

" *Bo-urn,* bound *of* land, tilth, *vi-nè-yard, nòne.*

He could not perceive that there are two fyllables wanting to complete the meaſure. Shakſpeare might have written :

> Bourn, *limit,* bound of land, tilth, vineyard, none.

P. 52.

Stephano here aſks Trinculo how he eſcaped, and the latter fays that he " fwam aſhore like a duck ;" adding, " I can fwim like a duck, I'll be fworn ;" than which nothing can be more fimple. Our Iriſh editor, however, in the *profundity* of his conceit, believes that " Trinculo is fpeaking of Caliban, and that we ſhould read—" *a'* can fwim, &c." than which nothing can be more abſurd.

P. 55.

All former editions reading

> ——moſt poor matters
> Point to rich ends. This my mean taſk

E

Would be as heavy to me as odious; but
The miſtreſs whom I ſerve quickens what's
  dead
And makes my labours pleaſures,—

our notable critic, for the improvement of the
metre, of which he is a complete judge, alters it
thus:

—moſt poor matters
Point to rich ends. This my mean taſk would
  be
As heavy to me as odious, but
The miſtreſs, &c.

And juſtifies the alteration by gravely telling us that
" our author and his contemporaries generally uſe
odious as a triſyllable." How then, will he tell us,
do *he* and *his* contemporaries uſe it?

It is evident that all we get by this capricious
change is a transfer to one line of the defect of another; at leaſt, to make any metre of the ſecond we
muſt read it thus:

" As heavy to me as *o-di-ous*, but ;"

as, the editor will undoubtedly pretend, our author
and his contemporaries generally pronounced it.

The inſertion of a ſingle ſyllable perfects the meaſure:

—moſt poor matters
Point to rich ends. This my mean taſk would
  be

As heavy to me as *'tis* odious; but
The miftrefs, &c.

P. 65.

Trin. The found is going away: let's follow it,
And after do our work.

Ste. Lead monfter, we'll follow,—I wou'd I
could fee this taborer: he lays it on.

Trin. Wilt come? I'll follow Stephano.

The words *Wilt come*, our fagacious editor believes, are addreffed to Stephano, who, from a de-
fire to fee the "taborer" lingers behind. Will you
come or not (fays Trinculo)? If you will not, *I'll
follow* Caliban without you."

Such an "*idle conjecture*" could only, one would
think, proceed from a dabbler equally ignorant of
our authors manner and unconfcious of his meaning.
It is, notwithftanding, very much in character. The
mufic is *going away*, and Stephano *lingers behind to
fee the performer*: this is *Paddy from Cork* with a
vengeance! Suppofe now we were to treat the paffage thus:

Ste. Lead monfter; we'll follow,—I would I
could fee this taborer: he lays it on. Wilt come?

Trin. I'll follow, Stephano.

It is Trinculo who "lingers behind."

E 2

TWO GENTLEMEN OF VERONA.

P. 120.

" O how this spring of love resembleth.

The editor has inserted both Mr. Tyrwhitts notes, without taking the least notice of the conclusive reply already made to the latter, and which it is unnecessary here to repeat. In return for this piece of candour, I shall only say that I do not in the least wonder to find *him* as ignorant of the principles of English orthography, as he is of the sense and language of the author he has had the presumption to think himself qualifyed to illustrate. Mr. Tyrwhitt was a man of indisputable learning and critical abilities; but, perhaps on that very account could not, like Cicero, be expected to

" ——follow any thing
That other men begin."

P. 133.

Pro. I'll die on him that says so but yourself.
Sil. That you are welcome.
Pro. That you are worthless.

Dr. Johnson, finding the measure defective, prefixed the word *No* to the latter hemistich, " But perhaps," says Mr. Malone, " the particle which he

has fupplyed is unneceffary. *Worthlefs* was, *I believe*, ufed as a trifyllable. See Mr. Tyrwhitt's
note, p. 120."

The gentleman, as his friend Bottom obferves,
has " a reafonable good ear in mufic," and " the
tongs and the bones" would be no improper accom-
paniment for fuch kind of harmony as he thus makes
of our all-excellent poets verfification. If *worthlefs*
be a trifyllable, it will be neceffary to infert a vowel
in order to receive the accent, which it muft be evident can neither fall upon *worth* nor *lefs*. One muft
therefore read :

That you are welcome.

That you are *worth-i-lefs*.

The editor feems to have acquired the fecret of
multiplying fyllables from a well-known ftory in Joe
Millers Jefts, where an equally ingenious Oxford
fcholar proves *two capons* to be *three*, and gets the
third for his pains.

They who look for information upon the fubject
in Mr. Tyrwhitts note will be as much difappointed
as that learned gentleman would have been furprifed
to find them fent thither for it.

MERRY WIVES OF WINDSOR.

P. 265.

Farewell, gentle *miftrefs* ; farewell Nan.

" *Miftrefs*" the editor fays, " is here ufed as a

trifyllable." The accent, of courſe, falls as uſual
upon the *ſecond :* e. g.

Farewell, gentle *miſ-tè-reſs* ; farewell Nan."

P. 261.

—to be compaſs'd like a good bilbo in the cir-
cumference of a peck, hilt to point.—

" Thus," ſays our editor, " the folio. The old
4to reads—of a *pack*, and perhaps rightly. Pediars
packs are ſometimes of ſuch a ſize as to admit of
Falſtaffs deſcription ; but who but a Lilliputian
could be " compaſſed in a *peck*."

O *feeble, ſhallow, profoundly ignorant* annotator !
It is the *bilbo*, not *Falſtaff*, that is " compaſſ'd in a
peck :" *He* was in a ſimilar condition in the *buck-
baſket*.

VOL. II.

MEASURE FOR MEASURE.

P. 101.

Ere twice the ſun hath made his daily greeting
To *yond* generation, you ſhall find, &c.

If the editor had followed the practice he imputes
to the editor of the ſecond folio, " of altering whatever he did not underſtand," we ſhould ſcarcely have
had a ſingle word of Shakſpeares left. It is there-

for rather fortunate that he has fo frequently af-
fected to underftand, not only what he was perfectly
ignorant of, but what in fact is utterly unintelligible
and abfolute nonfenfe.

Yond, in the above paffage, being an evident mifprint for *the under*, which had been written in the
copy *Yᵉ vnd'*, and is requifite both to the fenfe and
to the metre, our notable Hibernian explains it
to mean " the *without* door generation." The
metre of the line will therefor be very properly in
unifon with the fenfe.

To yond *ge-ne-ra-ti-on*, you fhall find.

P. 140.

And live if *not* then thou art doom'd to die :—
" *if* not,] Old copy—*no*. Corrected in the *fecond
folio.*"

The *fecond folio*, now under my eye, does not dif-
fer from the *firft*. Is this a fpecimen of the editors
accuracy or of his veracity?

MUCH ADO ABOUT NOTHING.

P. 269.

Leon. What do you mean my lord?
Claud. Not to be marry'd,
Not to knit my foul to an approve a wanton.
Leon. Dear my lord, if you in your own proof.

Thefe lines have been differently regulated; but

let that pafs : " *Dear*," our editor fays, " like *door*, *fire*, *hour*, and *many fimilar words*, is here ufed as a diffyllable. " We muft therefor read :

De-àr, my lord, if you, in your own proof :

which, it muft be confeffed, is one of the beft diffyllable lines throughout this harmonious edition.

LOVES LABOUR LOST.

P. 414.

Taffata phrafes, filken terms precife,
   Three-pil'd hyperboles, fpruce *affection*,
Figures pedantical, thefe fummer-flies
   Have blown me full of maggot *oftentation*.

" The modern editors," it feems, " read *affectation*;" but " there is no need of change. The word was ufed by our author and his contemporaries, as a quadrifyllable."

In the Devils name (God forgive me for fwearing !) what has the number of fyllables to do here ? It is the *rime* we are at a lofs for, not the *metre*. Surely, furely, if ever man was peculiarly difqualifyed by nature for an editor of Shakfpeare, or, in fhort, for a reader of poetry, it was this identical Mr. Malone ! Could it have been imagined that a writer in the eighteenth century would be fo *profoundly ignorant* of the commoneft rules of verfification, fo totally deſtitute of every idea of harmony and arithmetic, as to propoſe ſuch a ſtanza as the following?

 Taf-fa-ta phraf-es, ſilk-en terms pre-ciſ*e*,
  Three-pil'd hy-per-bo-les, ſpruce *af-fec-ti-òn*,
 Fi-gures pe-dan-ti-cal; theſe ſum-mer flies,
  Have blown me full of mag-got *oſ-ten-tà-ti-on*.

Perhaps, however, he will contend that *hyperboles* is a triſyllable, as nothing can be improbable, in reference to ſuch a genius, on the ſcore of abſurdity. Let it be ſo, it will make no ſort of difference:

 Three-pil'd *hy-per-boles*, ſpruce *af-fec-ti-òn*.

Only, in the one caſe, we ſee that *on* will be the rime to *ātion*; in the other, * īon*.

MIDSUMMER NIGHTS DREAM.

P. 459.

——Are you not he
That fright the maidens of the villagery;
Skim milk; and ſometimes labour in the quern,
And bootleſs make the breathleſs houſewife
 churn.

 " Perhaps," obſerves our ſagacious editor, " the conſtruction is—and ſometimes make the breathleſs houſewife labour in the quern, and bootleſs churn. This," he adds, " would obviate the objection made

(42)

by Dr. Johnſon, viz. that " the mention of the mill
ſeems out of place, for ſhe is not now telling the
good but the evil that he does." Such a conſtruction may be perfectly natural to the maker, whoſe
ideas ſeem to ſport in a moſt lovely confuſion, but
how is it poſſible for any other perſon to approve it?
Nothing can be more eaſy and intelligible than the
paſſage as it now ſtands ; and the objection taken by
Dr. Johnſon does not ſeem well founded : as the
fairy may have enumerated miſchievous acts *only*.
Pucks labour in the quern might be either to diſturb
the family with the noiſe, or, if he actually ground
the corn, when it was not wanted, or to throw the
flour about the houſe.

P. 464.

The human mortals want their winter here.

The poſition too haſtily advanced by Mr. Steevens
of the mortality of fairies has been ſo fully and completely refuted, that I do not at all wonder to find our
preſent candid and liberal editor continuing that
gentlemans note, tho' I own I am not a little ſur-
priſed to ſee the ſwaggering comment in the edition
of 1785 reduced to half a dozen words—

" See the *Faery Queen* B. II. c. 10 ; and Wartons OBSERVATIONS on Spenſer, vol. i. p. 55.
REED."

And why not likewiſe to " Tickell's poem, called
Kenſington Gardens," which was to ſhew " that the

opinion prevailed in the prefent century?"* But
the reduction and omiffion are fufficient to prove
that our modeft editor was himfelf convinced of the
fallacy of Mr. Steevens's affertion, and Mr. Reeds
authorities, though he has not had the candour to
acknowledge it. See the *Quip Modeft.* pp. 11. 33.

The paffage there quoted from Ariofto is thus
tranflated by Sir J. Harington:

"But (either auncient folke beleeu'd a lie,
"Or this is true) a *fayrie cannot die.*"

The following inftances, from this very play, were
accidentally omited:

"But *fhe, being mortal,* of that boy did die."

"I am a *fpirit* of no common fort."

If ever any pofition was or can be demonftrated
by literary evidence it is that the fairies of Shakfpeare
were not fubject to mortality. There is no evidence whatever on the other fide.

---

* This poem is printed in Dodfleys Collection, of which the
editor or revifer of the edition of 1785 had been a very few years
before employed in the republication. He muft therefor know that
it proved the direct reverfe of that for which he refered to it, and
confequently that he was afferting an untruth.

I fhould like to know from the gentleman concerned, or any
other able cafuift, the exact difference between afferting that a book
proves what the afferter knows it difproves, and producing, like
Lauder, fuppofititious extracts for the purpofe.

P. 499.

So, with two feeming bodies, but one heart
Two of the firft, like coats in heraldry,
Due but to one, and crowned with one creft.

" According to the rules of heraldry," it is the
editors note, " the *firft* houfe only, (e. g. a father
who has a fon living, or an elder brother as diftinguifhed from a younger,) has a right to bear the family coat. The fon's coat is diftinguifhed from the
father's by a label ; the younger brother's from the
elder's by a mullet. The fame creft is common to
both. Helena therefore means to fay, that fhe and
her friends were as clofely united, as much as *one*
perfon, as if they were *both of the firft houfe*; as if
they both had the privilege *due but to one* perfon,
(viz. to him of the firft houfe,) the right of bearing
the family coat without any diftinguifhing mark."
Every reader of this incomparable edition will
have frequent occafion to obferve that the editor
" draweth out the thread of his verbofity finer than
the ftaple of his argument." The prefent inftance,
indeed, is nothing in comparifon to pages of inanity
with which the work abounds, and which, on account of their " true no-meaning," are actually incapable of refutation or difcuffion. What, in the
name of Shakfpeare, of fenfe or reafon, has either *the*
father or *his eldeft fon* to do with the paffage in quef-

tion? The *two feeming bodies* united by *one heart* are refembled to *coats in heraldry, crowned with one creft.* And this happens either where the *heir* keeps his *paternal* and *maternal* coats, or *the hufband his own* and *his wifes,* in *feparate fhields,* as is done on the continent; or, as at prefent with us, in the quarterings of the fame fhield; in both cafes there are *two coats, due but to one, and crowned with one creft :* which is clearly the authors allufion. But I am forry to add that he muft have entirely mifunderftood, fince he has fo ftrangely mifapplyed, the expreffion, *Two of the firft*; which, in heraldical jargon, always means *two* objects *of the firft* colour mentioned; that is the *field.* For inftance : in blazoning a coat they will fay, *Argent,* upon a feffe *gules, two* mullets *of the firft,* that is, *argent,* the colour of the *field.* Thefe words are therefor a melancholy proof that our great author fometimes retained the phrafe after he had loft the idea, or up the former without fufficient precaution as to the latter. It is not indeed the only one; but " *quandoque bonus dormitat Homerus.*" With refpect to the note, as it is the offspring of *ignorance,* it becomes naturally the parent of *contempt.*

P. 473.

I know a bank *where* the wild thyme blows.

" *Where,*" Mr. Malone informs us, " is here

uſed as a diſſyllable. The modern editors," he ſays, unneceſſarily read—*whereon.*"

We muſt therefor, it ſeems, neceſſarily read:

" I know a bank *whe-àr* the wild thyme blows.

This, to be ſure, is no deſpicable line; Mr. Malone is a very pretty harmoniſt, in his way. But, if we muſt have a diſſyllable, why not *bank?*

" I know a *bà-ank* where the wild thyme blows."

Or *thyme,* ſtill better, as old Geoffrey might have had it?

" I know a bank where the wild *thymé* blows."

VOL. III.

MERCHANT OF VENICE.

P. 25.

—*away,* ſays the fiend, *for the heavens;* rouſe up a brave mind and run.

Away for the heavens, that is, as our editor explains it, " *Begone to the heavens.*" Now was it poſſible to imagine that a man who has been labouring for eight years, " with unceaſing ſolicitude, to give a faithful and correct edition of Shakſpeare" ſhould be ſo *profoundly* and completely *ignorant* of his meaning in this very fimple paffage? Can any thing be fo unnatural and abfurd as for the Devil to advife the perfon he is tempting to *go to heaven?* But why *to the heavens?* or how get thither? Mr. Malone, it is believed, will find the journey fome-what more difficult than he feems to apprehend it would have been to honeft Launcelot. In the mean time, every one, but this floundering commen-tator, knows that *for the heavens* is nothing more than an adjuration, or, as we now fay, *for the hea-vens fake.*

P. 33.

If a Chriftian *do* not play the knave, and get thee, I am much deceived.

" If a Chriftian (fays Launcelot, on receiving a love-letter for Lorenzo,) do not play the knave, and carry thee away from thy fathers houfe, I am much deceived." Such is the ingenious editors explana-tion, which he " would not have attempted of fo eafy a paffage, if the ignorant editor of the fecond folio, thinking probably that the word *get* muft neceffarily mean *beget*, had not altered the text, and fubftituted *did* in the place of *do*, in which he has been copied by every fubfequent editor." Every fubfequent edi-tor muft therefor be, at leaft, equally ignorant ; and I dare fay, if Mr. Malone is to be the judge, there never was editor, commentator or critic of Shak-fpeare who had a grain of fenfe befide himfelf. A

refutation cannot be expected of fuch peculiar abfurdity. " Launcelot," he fays, " is not talking about
Jeffica's father, but about her future hufband." But
how does he know this? who told him fo? can he
be better acquainted with the fubject of Launcelots
converfation than the man himfelf? He is aware, at
the fame time, that, in a fubfequent fcene, he fays to
Jeffica, " Marry, you may partly hope your *father got
you not*;" but he is now, it feems, on another fubject. That, however, is but the idle opinion of Mr.
Malone; the editor of the fecond folio, and all his
fucceffors, and, I will venture to add, Shakfpeare
himfelf, and all his readers, think very differently.

P. 38.

Shut *doors* after you : faft bind, faft find.

Former editors had fupplyed a fyllable, which is
equally neceffary to the fenfe and to the metre. But
the delicate ear and critical acumen of their Hibernian fucceffor have enabled him to difcover that
" *doors* is here ufed as a diffyllable." A previous
acquaintance with the Irifh howl muft be of infinite
fervice in the perufal of this harmonious edition.

Ibi.

How like a *younker*, and a prodigal.

This elegant and judicious emendation of the old
copies, which read *younger*, was made by Mr. Rowe.
Our more ingenious editor, however, with becoming

diffidence and profound knowlege, doubts " whether *younker* was a word of our authors time." It, however, happens, a little unluckily, not only to be a word of our authors time, but to be elfewhere ufed by our author himfelf. " What !" fays Falftaff, in the *Second part of King Henry IV.* " will you make a *younker* of me ?" Again in the *Third part of K. Henry VI.*

Trim'd like a *younker* prancing to his love.

If he has elfewhere doubted of his doubt, it only proves how little he is any where to be depended on.

P. 59.

For fear I furfeit !
  Baff. What find I *here.*

" The latter word is here employed as a diffyllable."

Of this there can be no doubt, as the line itfelf will prove :

For fear I furfeit.
          What find I *he-àr.*

P. 92.

As far as Belmont.
  Jef. In fuch a night, did
Young Lorenzo *fwear* he lov'd her well.

G

" *Swear* is here, as in many other places, a diffyllable."

This as ufual is confirmed by the metre :

As fār as Bēlmont.   In fŭch ā nĭght did
Young Lō-rĕn-zō fwĕ-ār he lōv'd her wēll.

Who can fay that our harmonious editor has not
employed his eight years labour to advantage when
he produces fuch lines as thefe ?

AS YOU LIKE IT.

P. 141.

———Now *go we in* content.

Go in we, an accidental tranfpofition of the firft
folio, being thus properly correčted in the fecond,
our editor, who will not allow that edition the merit
or liberty of correčting the moft glaring typographi-
cal blunder, is " not fure that the tranfpofition is
neceffary ;" for, as he fagaciously obferves, " our
author *might* have ufed *content* as an *adječtive :*"
Whence, I prefume, we muft neceffarily infer that
the correčtion has rendered it a *fubftantive, pronoun,
verb, participle, adverb, conjunčtion, prepofition* or *in-
terječtion.* He feems a very pretty grammarian.

P. 145.

The body of *country*, city, court.

Every one who has either ear or eye, will inftantly perceive here the want of a fyllable, which was fupplyed by the editor of the fecond folio, who reads

The body of *the* country, city, court;

a reading which is effential to the fenfe and meafure of the verfe, and which one may therefor reckon indifputably Shakfpeares. The prefent editor, however, who is in fact, what he would have the other thought to be, " utterly ignorant of our authors phrafeology and metre," omits the article, under pretence that " *Country* is here ufed as a *trifyllable.*" To reafon with a man who has no more ear for poetry than Dr. Johnfon had for mufic, and he fcarcely " knew a *drum* from a *trumpet*, or a *bagpipe* from a *guitar*," would be abfurd: every other perfon will fee it was utterly impoffible for Shakfpeare to write fuch a line as this, or indeed for any one but Mr. Malone to conceive it:

" The body of *coun-tè-ry*, city, court.

What a pity it is that the public cannot have the pleafure of hearing Mr. Malone read his own text ! I fay *pleafure*, becaufe undoubtedly it would be a moft laughable performance.

P. 195.

Over the wretched ? What though you have *mo* beauty.

The old copies reading—no *beauty*, the editor

will have it to be a mifprint for *mo*, or *more*, as he has every where elfe thought proper to write it. This, he fays, " appears clearly from the paffage in Lodge's *Rofalynde*, which Shakfpeare has here imitated :—" Becaufe *thou art beautiful*, be not fo coy, &c." A paffage which, as it contains neither *no* nor *mo*, can not certainly prove what it is brought to do. The conftruction adopted by this penetrating critic is that though a *woman* has *more* beauty than her *lover* fhe is not on that account to infult him : an idea which one can eafily fuppofe never entered into any head but his own ; one would not, therefor, wifh to deprive the prefent edition of an emendation fo worthy of it. But, however, Mr. Malone may read, his author certainly wrote

Over the wretched? what though you have beauty.

He could not perceive that *no* or *mo* was as injurious to the metre, as his quotation from Lodge might have led him to fufpect it was to the fenfe : though I believe he underftands both equally well. But, I well know that " my learned friend is above taking notice of fuch flender criticifm."

P. 205.

——I will *weep* for nothing *like Diana in the fountain*,

Our perspicacious editor had some years ago conjectured that these words had an allusion to some well-known conduit ; he has since found his conjecture confirmed, and elsewhere observed " that our author *without doubt* alluded to the ancient Cross in Cheapside," in which was an alabaster image of Diana, and water prilling *from her naked breasts.*" So that, unfortunately, the very instance which he has adduced in confirmation of the above sagacious conjecture totally destroys it ; unless the *tears* of his Cheapside Diana flowed from her *breasts*, instead of her *eyes*. This would have done well enough in Dublin.

P. 214.

> Ah, *sir*, a body would think this was well counterfeited.

" The old copy reads—Ah, *Sirra*, &c. Corrected by the editor of the *second* folio."

It ought, indeed, to have been so corrected by that editor : but the fact is that the second folio reads—Ah, *Sirra.*

TAMING OF THE SHREW.

P. 258.

Vincentio's son brought up in Florence.

" Vincentio's" according to Mr. Malone, " is

here ufed as a quadrifyllable. Mr. Pope " he adds,
" not perceiving this, unneceffarily reada.—Vincentio *his* fon, which has been too haftily adopted by
the fubfequent editors."

Mr. Malone, no doubt, is able to perceive a great
many things which neither Mr. Pope nor any body
elfe would dream of ; though, if Mr. Pope did not
perceive that a *word of four fyllables* was a *word of
four fyllables*, he muft have been a more extraordinary perfon than he is generally reputed. No, no,
Mr. Malone, it was not becaufe he did not perceive
Vincentio's to be ufed as a quadrifyllable, that he
read *Vincentio his*, but becaufe, not having had the
advantage of an Irifh education, he perceived that
fuch a line as the following could not have been
written by Shakfpeare :

Vin-cĕn-ti-ō's fon, brōught up īn Florĕnee.

Whatever people may choofe to fay of Mr. Malones edition, no one will deny him the exclufive
merit of deforming his authors verfe in the moft ri-
diculous and afinine manner poffible.

P. 295.

But, wrangling pedant, this is."

" Probably," the editor admits, " our author
wrote—this *lady* is, which," he fays, " completes
the metre, *wrangling* being ufed as a trifyllable.'

Now, in my humble opinion, it rather completes the evidence that the editor does not know what metre is. He fhould have accented his lines. What delectable harmony is here!

But, wrāng-gle-īng pedānt, this lady is.

There is a poem, intitled *Teifa*, which was publifhed a few years ago, entirely written in this way, and on that account a fort of curiofity. If it had not born the name of the author *(Anna Fifher)* and been upon a different fubject, I fhould have been pofitive that it was the production of our mufical editor. The faid poem, however, and his own Shakfpeare are, fo far as I know, the only fpecimens of this kind of metre extant either in the Englifh or any other language.

P. 315.

Where be thefe knaves? What no man at *door*.

" *Door* is here, and in other places, ufed as a dif-fyllable." Right; you have told us fo once before: let us therefor read the line, as it fhould be, in the Irifh way:

$$\overset{1}{\text{Where}} \overset{2}{\text{be}} \overset{3}{\text{thefe}} \overset{4}{\text{knaves}} ? \overset{5}{\text{What}} \overset{6}{\text{no}} \overset{7}{\text{man}} \overset{8}{\text{at}} \overset{9}{\text{do-}}\overset{10}{\overline{oor}}.$$

A dealer in diffyllables, poffeffed of the flighteft notion of harmony, would rather have made one of *knaves*; but an editor of common fenfe would read—the *door*.

PERICLES.

P. 556.

To pleafe the fool and death.

" The *Fool* and *Death*," Mr. Malone obferves, " were principal perfonages in the old *Moralities*." Mr. Malone is hereby called upon to mention one fingle Morality in which there is any fuch character as either *the Fool* or *Death*. If he can not, what are we to think of the morality of Mr. Malone?

V O L.   IV.

TWELFTH NIGHT.

P. 25.

With adoration's fertile tears.

" Tears," the editor fays, " is here ufed as a *dif-fyllable*;" and diffyllables are the moft convenient things in the world for patching up a broken verfe. Now, what, for inftance, can run more fmoothly than the following?

With ā-do-rā-ti-ōns fer-tīle te-ārs.

Ah, to be fure Mr. Malone is not a very good judge of harmony; to be fure he isn't !

P. 42.

Mar. My purpofe is indeed a horfe of that colour.

Sir And. And your horfe now would make
him an afs.

Mar. Afs, I doubt not.

Mr. Tyrwhitt believing that this conceit, which,
though bad enough, fhews, he thought, too quick an
apprehenfion for *fir Andrew*, fhould be given to *fir
Toby*; " An anonymous writer" afks, if the ingenious
critic imagined it " probable that Maria would call
fir Toby," whom, according to his own account, *fhe
adored*, an *afs*; upon which our truly affable and
diffident Hibernian, after premifing that his " learned
friend is above taking notice of fuch flender criticifm," roundly afferts that " Maria is not fpeaking of
fir Andrew, or fir Toby, but of *Malvolio!*" I fhould
infult the reader by defcending to refute an affertion
fo wantonly confident, and extravagantly abfurd.

P. 37.

And thanks, and ever thanks : Oft good turns.

Theobald inferted the fecond *thanks*, and added
likewife the word *and* to perfect the metre. Mr.
Malone, who is a much better judge of metre, fuf-
fers the former word to remain, but rejects the lat-

ter; having no doubt that *turns* was ufed as a *dif-syllable*. We muft therefor take care to read:

And thanks, and ever thanks: oft good *tu-ùrns*.

But why, Mr. Malone, fhould not *good* be a diffyllable, fince a diffyllable there muft be, as well as *turns*, and then, you fee, we fhall have no need of interpolating the *true original reading* of the *only ancien, authentic copy?*

WINTERS TALE.

P. 138.

Mr. Malone reads

———(for cogitation
Refides not in that man that does not think)

which being, as Fabian fays, " exceeding good fenfe-lefs," is judicioufly prefered to the correction of former editors:

———that does not think *it*.

This is not, however, as he afferts, the reading of the fecond folio. But certainly it ought to have been fo, which, in Irifh, may be the fame thing.

P. 164.

The pretty dimples of his chin, and cheek, his fmiles.

Dimples, according to our metrical Procruftes, as well as *of his*, is here employed as a *monofyllable*; which it muft be confeffed will make one of the prettyeft namby pamby lines that we can any where meet with.

> The pretty *dimp's of's* chin, and cheek, his fmiles.

Shakfpeare had no conception of thefe little Malonian beauties: he only wrote the line thus:

> The pretty dimples of his cheek, his fmiles;

leaving it for fuch fuperior geniufes as Mr. Malone to improve and finifh off.

P. 200.

> Burn hotter than my faith.
> *Per.* O but fir.

The editor of the fecond folio, who, ignorant as he was, feems to have had the ufe of his ears, eyes, and fingers, reads—

> O but *dear* fir.

This addition, however, our infallible metre-mafter pronounces unneceffary, " *burn* in the preceding hemiftic being," he fays, " ufed as a *diffyllable*." A *diffyllable!* nay then, all will be right enough, as we have only to read this moft beautiful and harmonious line:

" *Bu-ùrn* hot-tèr than mỳ faith. O but fĭr.

Ah, well! and who finds fault with it? For

" Dare you think your clumſy lugs ſo proper
    to decide as

" The *delicate ears* of *juſtice Midas ?*"

P. 242.

Here where we are.
Leon. The bleſſed Gods.

" Unleſs both *here* and *where* were employed as
diſſyllables, the metre is defective." O by all means
let them be employed as diſſyllables : they are moſt
uſeful and excellent things, and make the ſweeteſt
verſification imaginable. For inſtance :

He-àr, whe-àr we arè. The bleſſed Gods.

Or thus, more ſoftly

He-rèe whe-rèe we are. The bleſſed Gods.

Here is again " employed as a diſſyllable in *Macbeth,* p. 270,

Who comes *he-ar ?* The worthy thane of Roſs.

KING JOHN.

P. 454.

Kneel thou down, Philip, but riſe more great.

" *More* is here uſed as a *diſſyllable.*"

To be fure it is: and this Mr. Tyrwhitt might have thought an additional proof that our poet " had not forgotten his Chaucer :"

Kneel thou down, Philip, but rife *moré* great.

What an admirable thing is it to have a delicate ear! A plain hobbling fellow unbleffed with that advantage would have only thought the little word *up* wanting, and fpoiled, of courfe, a moft excellent mono-diffyllable.

P. 468.

It lies as fightly on the back of him
As great Alcides' *fhoes* upon an afs :

" i. e. upon the hoofs of an afs."

This comment is at leaft in unifon with the text. The idea of Hercules's *fhoes (N. B.* Hercules wore no fhoes) *lying* upon the *hoofs* of an *afs* is every way worthy of the ingenious Hibernian, from whom alone it could proceed.

VOL. V.

KING RICHARD II.

P. 46.

My lord, my anfwer is—to Lancafter.

The editors note on this paffage has been already

refuted; but if ignorance would fuffer him to perceive his error, obftinacy would not permit him to
confefs it.

P. 72.

I would the plants thou graft'ft may never grow.
 Gard. Poor queen! fo that thy ftate might
  be no worfe,
I would my fkill were fubject to thy curfe.

" An *anonymous writer* fuggefts that the queen
perhaps meant to wifh him childlefs. The gardeners anfwer fhews that this was not the authors
meaning."

The gardeners anfwer fhews no fuch thing : he
merely purfues the allufion.

FIRST PART OF KING HENRY IV.

P. 114.

Mordake earl of Fife, and eldeft fon.

" The word *earl*," our editor tells us, " is here
ufed as a *diffyllable*;" but " Mr. Pope, not perceiving this," reads—*the* earl.

" Mordake *e-àrl* of Fife, and eldeft fon.

Mr. Pope could no more have conceived Shakfpeare
capable of writing fuch a line, than he could have

written it himfelf : thefe difcoveries were referved
for a fecond-fighted Hibernian.

P. 142.

Fal. A baftard fon of the kings ?

Dr. Johnfon, having obferved that the improbability of this fcene is fcarcely balanced by the humour, our Irifh editor perceives no improbability ;
afferting roundly that Falftaff does NOT miftake the
prince for a baftard of the kings, but means to inform him at once that he knows him and Poins, notwithftanding their difguife.

The text, which is too plain to be mifunderftood
by a reader of common fenfe, will fpeak for itfelf,
and clearly prove that neither Falftaff nor the hoftefs
knows the prince till he fays he is " come to draw
him out by the ears." Falftaff himfelf allows that
he did not know the prince was within hearing :
but this perfpicacious critic, who can fee into the
midft of a millftone, would be thought to know
what paffes better than either Falftaff, or Falftaffs
creator.

P. 162.

Eaftcheap. A room in the boars head tavern.

" Shakfpeare," fays the editor, " has hung up a
fign that he faw daily ; for the *Boars head* tavern

was very near Blackfriars playhouſe. See Stows Survey, 4to. 1618. p. 686.

No doubt there might be many ſigns of the *Boars head*, in and about London, beſides that in Eaſt-cheap; but why need Shakſpeare be at the trouble of carrying a ſign from Blackfriars and hanging it up in Eaſtcheap, where, he muſt know, it exiſted already? If the *Boars head* were not the ſign of the *Boars head Tavern*, in Eaſtcheap, let the editor tell us what it was. If it were not, Shakſpeare might have looked long enough about Blackfriars playhouſe before he had found either the *Boars head* or the *Boars head Tavern*. The ſign which Stow mentions was a *Beares head*, and he ſpeaks of it—not as hanging at the time he wrote, but—as having formerly been one of the ſigns of the ſtew-houſes, which had been long ſuppreſſed, and which, every one knows, were not near Blackfriars playhouſe. See his *Survay*, 1598, p. 332.

P. 188.

> *Fal.* I deny your *major*: if you will deny the *ſheriff*, ſo.

" An anonymous writer," we are informed, " ſuppoſes, that Falſtaff here intends a quibble. *Major*, which ſheriff brought to his mind, ſignifies as well one of the parts of a logical propoſition, as the principal officer of a corporation."—" To render this fuppofition probable," fays the editor, " it fhould be proved, that the mayor of a corporation was called in Shakfpeares time *ma-jor.*"

The fuppofition would appear fufficiently probable although the pronunciation contended for could not be eftablifhed by a quotation. Every one knows that *Mayor* is *Major* in Latin, which would be enough for the prefent purpofe. The proof required can only be neceffary for one who has every where betrayed the *profoundeft ignorance* of his authors language, and who pretends to have collated editions, which, if we may judge from the blunders of his own, he has never looked into. The identical pronunciation in queftion happens, fortunately enough, to be preferved in one of our authors own plays, the *Firft part of K. Henry VI.* as printed in the " only ancient authentic edition," the folio of 1623.

> *Major* farewell : thou doo'ft but what thou may'ft.

KING HENRY V.

P. 508.

Flu. Gots ploot ! up to the preaches, &c.

Nothing need or can be added to what has been already urged againft this corrupted text and prevaricating comment. See the *Quip Modeft,* &c. p. 27.

How unfortunate is it, how injurious to the me-

I

mory of this great and admirable writer, that his beſt ſcenes ſhould be thus mangled and deformed by a reſtoration, equally impudent and fooliſh, of what he himſelf has thought fit to alter or reject! Such conduct deſerves a *pillory* rather than a *pamphlet*.

P. 584.

Toward Calais : grant him *there* ; *there* ſeen.

" If *Toward*," the editor obſerves, " be not abbreviated, our author with his accuſtomed licence uſes one of theſe words as a diſſyllable, while to the other he aſſigns only its due length."

Arrah! my dear, this will be after mending the matter by making bad worſe. The line already wants *one* ſyllable, if *toward* be abbreviated it will want *two*—and then there will be ten. So that take *two* from *ten*, and there remains *ten*. Our editor is a notable arithmetician in his way: he can multiply one ſyllable into two or three, reduce two or three to one, and play a thouſand ſuch tricks, which neither Cocker nor Breſlaw ever once dreamt of. I am apt to ſuſpect, however, after all, that the above obſervation labours under a capital error of the preſs ; and that, inſtead of the words " our *author* with his accuſtomed *licence*," we ſhould read " our *editor* with his accuſtomed *ignorance*."

VOL. VI.

FIRST PART OF KING HENRY VI.

P. 22.

Glofter, we'll meet to thy coft, be fure.

" The latter word" being " here ufed as a diffyl-lable," we are to read the line thus :

Glof-ter, we'll meet to thy coft be *fu-ùre*,

than which nothing can be more Malonious—har-monious I would fay.

P. 30.

A ftatelier pyramis to her I'll rear
Than Rhodope's *or* Memphis ever was.

Mr. Steevens having propofed to read—of *Memphis*, as Shakfpeare unqueftionably wrote, this faga-çious Hibernian obferves " Rhodope was of *Thrace*, not of *Memphis*." Well ! and whoever fuppofed fhe was of *Memphis* ? But her *pyramis* was there ; which is fufficient authority for the correction.

P. 44.

Enter Mortimer.

Mr. Steevens, from the MS. notes of Mr. Edwards, having obferved " that Shakfpeare has varied from the truth of hiftory, to introduce this fcene between Mortimer and Richard Plantagenet," " a half-informed *Remarker* on this note" (they are the words of the gentle Edmond) " feems to think that he has totally over-turned it, by quoting the following paffage from Hall's *Chronicle :* " During which parliament [held in the third year of Henry VI. 1425.] came to London Peter Duke of Quimber,—which of the Duke of Exeter, &c. was highly fefted.—During which feafon Edmond Mortymer, the laft Erle of Marche of that name, (whiche long tyme had bene reftrayned from hys liberty and finally waxed lame) difceafed without yffue, whofe inheritance defcended to Lord Richard Plantagenet," &c. as if a circumftance which Hall has mentioned to mark the *time* of Mortimer's death, neceffarily afcertained the *place* where it happened alfo. The fact is, that this Edmund Mortimer did *not* die in London, but at Trim in Ireland." So far, fo good.

This tefty critic feems to fmart fo much from fome corrections of that fame " half-informed *Remarker*," that he may be readily allowed to avail himfelf of every opportunity of abufing him, particularly where he happens to anticipate a quotation which an all-informed editor would have been glad to produce. The paffage in Hall (and it is copyed by Hollinfhed) would be fufficient, it was faid, to juftify Shakfpeare " even if the fact were otherwife;" and

so it undoubtedly is, notwithstanding either the great
learning or little scurrility of Edmond Malone.
The historian does not, to be sure, expressly say
that the Earl of March dyed in the *Tower*; but no
person of common sense can think that he meant to
relate an event which happened to a *found, free man*
in *Ireland*, as happening to a *lame prisoner* during the
time a particular person was feasting in *London*. In
fact, he *does* say that this nobleman *dyed in prison*, and
that by such prison he meant either the *Tower*, or
some place of confinement at no great distance,
is almost certain, not only from the circumstance
already mentioned, but from a passage in the preceding part of his book, where he expressly tells us
that " the Erle of Marche was euer *kepte in the
courte* vnder such a keper that he could nether doo
or attempte any thyng agaynste the king without his
knowledge, and dyed without issue." If he did not
mean the *Tower*, let Mr. Malone say what prison he
did mean. To what purpose is it that the actual
truth was otherwise? Our author had neither *Rymer*, nor *Dugdale*, nor *Sandford*, to consult, and it
cannot surely be expected that he should have gone
to examine the record office: He naturally took for
fact what he found in *History*, and if the historian
were but *half-informed*, how could he help it? He
was writing a play, not a chronicle. I know, much
better, I am persuaded, than Mr. Malone, how little
either Hall or Hollinshed is to be depended on in

matter of fact. Is the death of Edmond Mortimer of greater confequence than the intended marriage of lady Bona, or the capture, imprifonment and efcape of K. Edward IV. both which are abfolutely fabulous and without the flighteft poffible foundation. And why is not Shakfpeare, who has adopted thefe two lying ftories, charged with having in thefe inftances " varyed from the truth of hiftory ?" The remark was natural enough to Mr. Edwards, who did not know what fort of hiftories our author confulted ; neither indeed is the editors defence of it otherwife, being a pedantic parade of hiftorical knowlege picked up for the occafion, to faften Shakfpeare with a charge which every one muft think frivolous, and which he knew to be unjuft.

SECOND PART OF K. HENRY VI.

P, 134.

She's tickled now, her fume needs no fpurs.

" *Tickled*," it feems, " is here ufed as a trifyllable. The editor of the fecond folio, *not perceiving this*, reads—" her fume can need no fpurs ;" in which he has been followed by all the fubfequent editors."

The editor of the fecond folio, then, has had the ufe of his ears, which is more than can be faid of his Hibernian fucceffor. It requires a certain degree of folly, peculiar to this all-accomplifhed critic, not to perceive—that whether *tickled* be a diffyllable, or a trifyllable or a quadrifyllable, cannot make the flight-eft difference; the defect of the line being in another quarter.—According to the hypothefis of our Bœotian editor, we ought to read the line as follows:

She's *tic-kle-èd* now, hèr fume needs no fpurs.

What a pity it is that Mr. Malone does not appear upon the ftage!

THIRD PART OF K. HENRY VI.

P. 267.

Prove it, *Henry*, and thou fhalt be king.

" *Henry*," being " frequently ufed by Shakfpeare and his contemporaries as a word of three fyllables," muft be thus pronounced:

Prove it, *He-nè-ry*, and thou fhalt be king.

P. 272.

When I return with victory *from* the field.

" Folio—*to* the field. The true reading is found in the old play."

The true reading is found in the fecond folio; which affords one out of many proofs that this edition is not what the editors malice or ignorance has chofen to reprefent it.

P. 276.

M.f. The queen with all the Northern earls
     and lords
Intend here to befiege you in this caftle.

" An anonymous Remarker," we are told, " very
confidently afferts that " this fcene, fo far as refpects
Yorks *oath* and *his refolution to break it*, proceeds
entirely from the authors imagination. His oath,"
however, " is in record, and what his *refolution* was
when he marched from London at the head of a
large body of men, and fent the meffage abovestated
to his fon, it is not very difficult to conjecture."

A little fuperficial reading, and a confummate
ftock of affurance authorife this hypercritical commentator to abufe what he does not underftand.
The " anonymous Remarker," confidently if it muft
be, afferts that the fcene in queftion, in which Edward and Richard perfuade their father to break his
oath, had no foundation in hiftory ; and gives this
reafon for it, that, " neither the Earl of March nor
Richard was then at Sandal ; the latter being likewife a mere child, fcarcely more than (if indeed fo
much as) nine years old :" in fact he was but juft
turned of eight. How, therefor, does the Irifh editor, with all his pitiful caviling and malignity, pick
out from thefe words that York had never taken an
oath ? And, though he and Warwick did leave Lon-

don with 5 or 6,000 men, and might fend a meffage to his fon to follow them, it was with the kings own authority, to fupprefs an infurrection againft the eftablifhed government : nor could either his attacking, or his defending himfelf againft, the queen or prince be any breach of his oath. So that the Remarkers affertion, however confident, is ftrictly true ; which is more than this ingenuous Hibernian can always fay of his own, which are at the fame time very feldom diftinguifhable by diffidence.

It is not true that the queen and prince were at York, nor do we find from any good authority that they were fent to by the King. Though, if they had been fent to, and, inftead of obeying the requifition, had employed themfelves in raifing a rebellion, it would have been perfectly confonant with the dukes oath and duty to have prevented or quelled it. But in fact, whatever concern the queen might have in the Yorkfhire infurrection, fhe did not return from Scotland till after the battle of Wakefield.

What fort of hiftories the Irifh editor confults I am at a lofs to imagine ; and as he does not choofe to cite them, I fhall for once follow his example. *

---

* I collect from another note (p. 321) where he fays that " neither of his daughters was married at the time when Warwick was in France negotiating a marriage between lady Bona and the king," that the learned gentleman is content either with the fame hiftorians whom Shakfpeare ufed, or with thofe who have followed them : Warwick *never* was in France for any fuch purpofe : as no one but fuch a " half-informed" note-writer can be ignorant.

K

The abfurd note at p. 278. being founded in grofs mifapprehenfion, or *profound ignorance*, is unworthy of more particular notice.

P. 289.

So many *years* ere I fhall fheer the fleece.

" Mr. Rowe," we are told, " changed *years to months*; which was followed by the fubfequent editors; and in the next line inferted the word *weeks*, not obferving that *hours* is ufed as a diffyllable. *Years*," it feems, " is in that line likewife ufed as a word of two fyllables."

The reafon of Mr. Rowes changing *years* to *months*, and inferting *weeks* was not, as this equally fuperficial and blundering commentator imagines, purely on account of the meafure, but becaufe the king has already mentioned *weeks* and *years*, and afterward enumerates *months*. Thefe two curious diffyllables it muft be confeffed, help the metre prodigiously: but, in fact, the editor fhould be expected to rehearfe his text to the purchafer, as no one will ever be able to read it without his inftructions. The line in queftion would feem to be accented thus :

So mi-nutes, *hou-ers*, days, months, and *ye-àrs*.

P. 360.

Now brother Richard, *lord* Haftings, and the reft.

One of the former commentators having, very judiciously, propofed to omit the word *lord*, our ingenious editor obferves that *brother*, like many fimilar words, is here ufed by Shakfpeare as a monofyllable, and the metre was to his ear perfect. He fhould rather have faid, that it is fo to his own: which indeed, I can as eafily believe as pardon; fince the gentleman unfortunately labours under a natural defect, to which whoever interpolated the word muft have been alfo fubject, though not in an equal degree. The ears of Shakfpeare were formed very differently from Mr. Malones. Obferve how fmoothly the verfe will run!

Now *brò'r Ri-chàrd*, lord Haftings, and the reft.

The editor is unable to perceive the confequences of his own fyftem. The luminous arrangement of his ideas is altogether wonderful!

K. RICHARD III.

P. 569.

When didft thou fleep when fuch a deed was done?

Q. Mar. When holy Harry dy'd, and my fweet fon.

" The editor of the fecond folio," fays our acute critic, " changed *When* to *Why*, which has been adopted by all the fubfequent editors ; though Margarets anfwer evidently refers to the word found in the original copy."

The editor of the fecond folio feems to have underftood his authors meaning, which is by no means the cafe with his " flimfy" antagonift. *Why* is " evidently" right. How happens it, exclaims the queen, that Heav'n flept when fuch a deed was done! Margaret, catching at the words *fuch a deed*, adds When holy Henry and my fon were murdered.

If *When* were right the queen would be guilty of a manifeft abfurdity, as the queftion would anfwer itfelf. But an Irifh editor muft have an Irifh text.

P. 588.

What heir of York is there alive, but we?
And who is Englands king, but great Yorks
heir?

" Richard," fays the editor, " afks this queftion in the plenitude of power, and no one dares to anfwer him. But they whom he addreffes, had they not been intimidated, might have told him, that there was a male heir of the houfe of York alive, who had a better claim to the throne than he ; Edward earl of Warwick the only fon of the ufurpers elder brother George duke of Clarence ; and Elizabeth, the eldeft daughter of Edward IV. and all her fifters, had a better title than either of them."

Either this frivolous commentator is " profoundly ignorant" of the hiftory of the monarch whom he choofes to call ufurper, or wilfully mifreprefents it. King Richard, it is well known, had as good a title to the crown as the late king William or queen Anne, or the reigning houfe of Hanover. The iffue of King Edward had been *baftardized*, the duke of Clarence *attainted*, and himfelf *declared the undoubted heir of Richard duke of York*, BY ACT OF PARLIA-MENT : and what better title has the prefent king? It might as well be faid that, when he, by his champion, challenged all the world to difpute his right, he did it " in the plentitude of power ;" and that they whom he addreffed, " had they not been intimidated, might have told him that there was a male heir of the houfe of ' STUART' alive, who had a better claim to the throne than he !" An act of parliament is of no more force in the 17th or 18th century than it was in the 15th.

VOL. VII.

CORIOLANUS.

P. 193.

" The etymology which Dr. Johnfon has given in his dictionary—" MALKIN, from *Mal* or *Mary*, and *kin*, the diminutive termination,"—is, I apprehend, erroneous." MALONE.

Mr. Malones apprehenſion ariſes from his ignorance of the Engliſh language. The diminutives
Wilkin, Tomkin, Jenkin, Perkin, Simkin, &c. &c.
ſufficiently corroborate Dr. Johnſons etymology;
and they who know to what the diminutive of *Margaret* has given a name can be at no loſs to account
for the reaſon of *Malkin* being degraded to ſignify a
mop of clouts, or a *ſcarecrow :* neither of which ſig-
nifications, by the way, has anything to do with the
text. But ſuch is the abſurd conſequence of an Iriſh
editor attempting the illuſtration of an Engliſh author.

P. 159.

Corioli.] As the editor makes an uncommon fuſs
with his pretenſions of adhering to the old copy, let
him give a reaſon why he has choſen to read *Corioli,*
not only in oppoſition to his original, but to Shakſpeares authority,—Norths *Plutarch.* This, however, is not mentioned as the only inſtance he has
given us of his want of truth, fidelity, candour, and
conſiſtency.

P. 220.

Sic. You ſhew too much of that.

" This ſpeech is given in the *old copy* to *Cominius.*
It was rightly attributed to *Sicinius* by Mr. *Theobald.*"

Having neither Theobalds edition nor the firſt

folio at prefent before me, I fhall leave the above
affertion to its credit. But this I can fay, that the
fecond folio, which, if it is not to be called an " old
copy," is clearly not a very modern one, gives the
fpeech to *Sicinius*; and I, for one, do not believe
that the firft gives it to any body elfe. If it does,
the fecond folio is good for fomething; which is
more than any one will be found to fay of Mr. Malones edition, at the end of a century and a half,
fhould it fo long have the unmerited good fortune to
efcape the figs and pepper to which it is deftined.

P. 237.

Becaufe that now it lies you on to fpeak,
To the people ; not by your own inftruction,
Nor by the matter which your heart prompts
    you,
But with fuch words that are but roted in
Your tongue, though but baftards and fyllables
Of no allowance to your bofoms truth.

The editor being as devoid of harmony as one of
the long ear'd fraternity, naturally thinks, if he be
capable of thinking,—for, as he elfewhere makes his
author obferve,

————cogitation
Refides not in the man who does not think,—

that all his readers muft be as defectively organized
as himfelf. How elfe could he have printed fuch

execrable hobbling lines as coming from Shakfpeare ?
He will not have fenfe to perceive the fuperiority of
the following arrangement ;—it is not intended for
him. To offer him harmonious verfes would be
literally throwing pearls to fwine.

> Becaufe
> That now it lies you on to fpeak to th' people,
> Not by your own inftruction, nor by th matter
> Which your heart prompts you to, but with
> fuch words
> That are but roted in your tongue, but baftards,
> Of no allowance to your bofoms truth.

Prompts you to is the reading of the fecond folio.
The words *Though* and *and fyllables* have been interpolated by fuch another editor as himfelf ; as they
only ferve to make nonfenfe of the paffage. But,
indeed, fenfe or nonfenfe, harmony or difcord, verfe
or profe are all the fame to him.

P. 283.

> If you have heard your general talk of Rome,
> And of his friends there, it is *lots* to *blanks*,
> My name hath touch'd your ears.

A *lot*, here; Dr. Johnfon fays, is a *prize*. It certainly is fo ; though our fagacious Hibernian believes
him miftaken. Menenius, he imagines, only means
to fay that it is more than an equal chance that his

name had touch'd their ears : which is precifely
the effect of Dr. Johnfons explanation. But, adds
he, if *lot* fignifyed *prize*, there being in every lottery
many more blanks than prizes, Menenius muft be
fuppofed to fay, that the chance of his name having
reached their ears was very fmall : a criticifm exactly calculated for the meridian of Tipperary. Menenius fays it is *prizes* to *blanks*, fomething to nothing, 20,000l. to a piece of wafte paper, &c. A
lot is what one *gains* in the lottery ; and our learned
editor, no doubt, if he got a blank, would fay he had
gain'd a *lofs*. Neither Shakfpeare, however, nor
Menenius was an Irifhman.

JULIUS CÆSAR.

P. 334.

Are then in council and the ftate of *a* man.

Such, it feems, is the reading of the elder copy.
" The editor of the fecond folio omitted the article,
probably from a miftaken notion concerning the
metre ; and all the fubfequent editors have adopted
his alteration. Many words of two fyllables," however, " are ufed by Shakfpeare as taking up the time
of only one ; as *whether, either, brother, lover, gentle, fpirit*; &c. and I fuppofe," concludes this profound critic, " *council* is fo ufed here."

There can be no occafion, I fhould think, to make

L

any remark upon a note of which the premiffes are
fo falfe, and the conclufion fo foolifh.   Neither our
author nor any other author in the world ever ufed
fuch words as *either*, *brother*, *lover*, *gentle*, *fpirit* as
monofyllables; and though *whether* is fometimes fo
contracted, the old copies on that occafion ufually
print *where*.   It is, in fhort, morally impoffible that
two fyllables fhould be no more than *one*.

P. 356.

——If this be known,
Caffius *or* Cæfar never fhall turn back,
For I will flay myfelf.

The editor believes that Shakfpeare wrote

Caffius *on* Cæfar never fhall turn back,

And fays, the next line ftrongly fupports this conjecture.   He muft mean, it is prefumed, in the Irifh
way; as a mere Englifh reader would conclude that
the next line totally deftroys it.   If, adds he, the
confpiracy was difcovered, and the affaffination of
Cæfar rendered impracticable by " *prevention*," Caffius could have no hope of being able to prevent
Cæfar from " turning back; and in all events this
confpirators " flaying himfelf" could not produce
that effect.

It is much to be lamented that the legiflature has
not prevented this mifconceiving, blundering fo-

reigner from difhonouring and debafing the margin
of Shakfpeare by fuch palpable abfurdities. Caffius
fays, if the plot be difcovered, at all events either he
or Cæfar fhall never return alive, for, if the latter
cannot be killed, he is determined to flay himfelf.
The fenfe is as plain, as the alternative is juft and
neceffary, or the propofed reading ignorant and abfurd.

P. 376.

Even at the bafe of Pompeys ftatue.

If *even*, fays the editor, be confidered as a monofyllable, the metre, of which to be fure he is an admirable judge, will be defective. But though it is
not our authors practice to make this adverb a diffyllable, yet clearly if we treat it as one, the defect is
removed, and the metre exactly fuited to " the delicate ears" of this Irifh Midas ; whofe admirers are
to read the line thus :

E-vēn ät thē bäfe ōf Pŏmpēys ftä-tūe.

P. 377.

For I have neither *writ*, nor words, nor worth.

The firft folio, by an evident blunder, having
writ, is followed by our congenial editor, who does
not like to fee a blunder corrected. *Wit*, the reading of the fecond folio, will receive the approbation
of every one who has fenfe.

L 2

P. 383.

Our beſt friends made, our means ſtretch'd *to
the utmoſt*.

We are indebted for the three laſt words to the
conceit of the preſent editor, who has had the modeſty to advance them to the honour of a place in
the text. The ſecond folio, from ſome good authority, no doubt, reads :

Our beſt friends made, *and* our *beſt* means
ſtretch'd *out*.

Which, whether he underſtand it or not, has an
evident and eaſy ſenſe, and is perfectly in our authors
manner.

————ſtretch'd to the utmoſt

is much too *Maloniſh* for ſo correct and elegant a
writer.

ANTONY AND CLEOPATRA.

P. 466.

Go to then ; your conſiderate ſtone.

Sir W. Blackſtone having remarked that the metre of this line is deficient, the editor, with his uſual
modeſty obſerves that " *Your*, like *hour*, is uſed as a
diſſyllable ; the metre therefore is not defective."

Defective? no, certainly; nothing can be more harmonious:

Go tō then; yōu-er cōn-ſi-dē-rate ſtōne.

However, as Enobarbus, to whom it belongs, generally ſpeaks in plain proſe, there is no occaſion for
any further attempt to harmonize it.

P. 474.

——Good night dear lady.——
Good night, ſir.

" Theſe laſt words, which in the only authentick
copy of this play are given to Antony, the *modern
editors*," according to Mr. Malone, " have aſſigned
to Octavia. I," however, he adds, " ſee no need
of change." He addreſſes himſelf to Cæſar, who immediately replies, *Good night*." The firſt of theſe
" *modern editors*" happens to be his old friend the
editor of the ſecond folio (which he pretends to have
collated with ſo much care), who appears, from this
and numberleſs other inſtances, to have had a copy
of the firſt folio corrected by the players who publiſhed it, or ſome other well-informed perſon. That
Mr. Malone ſees " no need of change" is the
ſtrongeſt poſſible reaſon for believing that a change
is abſolutely neceſſary. And ſo it certainly is: Antony has already ſaid " Good night, ſir," to Cæſar,
in the three firſt words of his ſpeech: the repetition
would be abſurd.

P. 479.

Ram thou thy *fruitful* tidings in mine ears,
That long time have been *barren.*

Though the first word is evidently a misprint for
Rain, as it has been given by Sir T. Hanmer and
others, the editor *suspects no corruption.* " The
term employed in the text," he says, " is much in
the style of the speaker ;" (what he means by that
is difficult to say ;) " and is supported *incontestably* by
a passage in *Julius Cæsar,*" which *incontestably* does
not support it at all, the idea being perfectly distinct.
The term employed, however, as well as the note
upon it, is much in the style of the editor ; and it
would be a pity to lose any opportunity of laughing
at his bulls and blunders; which, it must be never-
theless admitted, are as impertinent in the margin
of Shakspeare as a buffoon would be in a church.

Ram is likewise a vulgar word, never used in our
authors plays, but once by Falstaff, where he de-
scribes his situation in the buck-basket. Though if,
in the *Tempest,* the negligence of a press-man had
left

——Heavens *ram* grace,

this judicious critic would have supported that authentic reading in the same way. For, as he has
elsewhere justly observed, " If such *capricious innovations* were to be admitted, every line in these plays

might be changed." Some people are too ignorant
to innovate.

P. 499.

Spake you of Cæfar? *How?* the nonpareil!

" *How*, I believe, was here printed by miftake
for *ho!*" MALONE.

It was not; and *ho*, which this ingenuous annotator found in the fecond folio, is nothing more than
an accidental tranfpofition of *oh*.

Oh Antony! *oh* thou Arabian bird!

The editor can pilfer, though he cannot praife.

P. 508.

Then, world, thou haft a pair of chaps no more,
And throw between them all the food thou haft,
They'll grind *the one* the other. Where's An-
tony?

Dr. Johnfons emendation certainly deferved a
place in the text; and a very flight alteration would
prevent its deftroying the metre, which any but our
afinego of an editor will inftantly perceive.

———grind *the one the other*———

will never do. The meafure is perfect in the old
reading, which requires only one fyllable for another.
Shakfpeare wrote :

They'll grind *each* other. Where is Antony?

P. 575.

Being fo *fruftrate*, tell him he mocks *us by*
The paufes that he makes.

The two laft words of the firft line are added by
the prefent Irifh editor, who obferves that " the defect of the metre," of which he knows as much as
a fuperannuated jack-afs, " fhews that fomething
was omitted." Former editors fupplyed the meafure by reading

Being fo fruftrate*d*, tell him he mocks ;

which, it muft be confeffed, does not afford an eafy
fenfe. Shakfpeare, however, would never have written the above hobbling line, which has no fort of
pretenfions to metre. We may read :

Being fo fruftrated, he mocks us by.

VOL. VIII.

TIMON OF ATHENS.

P. 27.

The ear, tafte, touch, *fmell, all* pleas'd from thy
table rife.

" *The ear*," it feems, " was intended to be contracted into one fyllable ; and *table* alfo was proba-

bly ufed as taking up only the time of a monofyllable." This nonfenfe is to juftify the retention of
all, which better judges had found it neceffary to
omit, or rather to change for *fmell*. Mr. Malone
reads the line thus, that is, if he can read at all :

> Th'ear, tafte, touch, fmell, all pleas'd from *thy*
> *tāil* rife.

P. 40.

The clamorous demands of *date*-broken bonds.

The old editions read :

> ——of *debt*, broken bonds.

Hanmer and others omit the fyllable, which the prefent editor has thus judiciously reftored; being unable to perceive that he was injuring the metre,
without improving the fenfe.

P. 52.

> ——This flave
> Unto *his honour* has my lords meat in him.

The modern editors have concurred in reading—

> Unto *this hour*—

as unqueftionably Shakfpeare wrote. But the corruption, being manifeft nonfenfe, is properly replaced
in the prefent text, where it will find nothing to put
it out of countenance.

M

P. 61.

The devil knew not what he did, when he made man politick; he crofs'd himfelf by't: and I cannot think but in the end, the villanies of man will fet him clear.

The meaning, as elucidated by this perfpicacious critic is as follows : *The devil did not know what he was about when he made man crafty and interefted; he thwarted himfelf by it; and I cannot but think that at laft the enormities of mankind will rife to fuch a height as to make even Satan himfelf, in comparifon appear* (what he would leaft of all wifh to be) *fpotlefs and innocent*; which feems much more obfcure than the text itfelf. The editor has omitted three very weak notes of Warburton, Johnfon and Tollett, to make way for his own nonfenfe; but why the paffage fhould have required a note, except to inform us that the commentator did not underftand it, is not eafy to conceive. The devils folly in making man politic is to appear in this, that he will at the long run be too many for his old mafter, and get free of his bonds. The villanies of man are to fet himfelf clear, not the devil, to whom he is, by ignorant en-thufiafts, fuppofed to be in thralldom.

P. 63.

Your mafters confidence was above mine,
Elfe, furely, his had equall'd.

Our modeſt Hibernian, after giving an interpretation, which he profeſſes to think wrong, becauſe " a ſhallow Remarker" has endeavoured to
repreſent it as unintelligible, allows it may be ſo to
him, as the wit of ſome men (meaning, of courſe, his
own) like Falſtaffs deſert " is too thick to ſhine, and
too heavy to mount." " This Remarker, however,"
he proceeds to relate, " *after a feeble attempt at jocularity*, and ſaying that he ſhall take no further notice
of this editors *ſee-ſaw conjeċtures*, with *great gra-
vity* propoſes a comment evidently formed on the
latter of them, as an original interpretation of *his
own*, on which the reader may *ſafely* rely."

Friend Butler ſomewhere tells us, there is no argument like matter of faċt : we ſhall preſently ſee
who is the *thief*.

In the edition of 1778, the latter of this ingenious
gentlemans " ſee-ſaw conjeċtures" is as follows :
" The paſſage however may be explained thus :——
His may refer to *mine* ; as if he had ſaid : Your
maſter's confidence was above *my maſters* ; elſe
ſurely *his*, i. e. the ſum *demanded from my maſter* (for
that is the laſt antecedent) had been equal to the
ſum *demanded from yours*."

The *Remark* is : " Your maſter, it ſeems, had
more confidence in lord Timon than mine, other-
wiſe, his (*i. e.* my maſters) debt (*i. e.* the ſum due to
him from Timon) would, certainly, have been as great
as your maſters (*i. e.* as the money which Timon owes

to your mafter); that is, my mafter, being as rich
as yours, could and would have advanced Timon as
large a fum as your mafter has advanced him, if he
(*i. e.* my mafter) had thought it prudent to do fo."

Very well: now comes " the true explication,"
which the editor fays he " alfo formerly propofed;"
an affertion, if he mean in the edition of 1778,
which is evidently untrue. The reader may com-
pare them.

" *His* may refer to *mine*. " It fhould feem that
the confidential friendfhip fubfifting between your
mafter and Timon was greater than that fubfifting
between Timon and my mafter; elfe furely *his* fum,
i. e. the fum *borrowed* from *my* mafter, [the laft
antecedent] had been as large as the fum *borrowed*
from yours."

It muft be perfectly clear, that the Remarker
could not be indebted to a note which, fo far as it is
intelligible, feems diametrically oppofite to his idea.
It is equally fo, that the editor has availed himfelf of
the above " fhallow" Remark, to vary the expreffion of his " fee-faw conjecture," and give it a fenfe
it would otherwife never have had. Q. E. D.

TROILUS AND CRESSIDA.

P. 145.

And fkill-lefs as unpractis'd infancy.

Dr. Johnfon fays that " Mr. Dryden, in his alteration of this play, has changed *ſkill-leſs* to *artleſs*, not for the better, becauſe *ſkill-leſs* refers to *ſkill* and *ſkilful*. " A very *fond* and *ſkill-leſs Remarker*, on this note," adds the editor, " aſks and does not *artleſs* refer to *art* and *artful*."

Without intereſting myſelf at all in what I do not profeſs to underſtand, I ſhall only beg leave to ſay that if Mr. Malone meant, by this piece of inſolent vulgarity, to aſſert that there was any ſuch queſtion in the " *Remarks on the laſt edition*, &c. 1785, the aſſertion is a groſs falſehood. He ſeems to commit forgery for the ſake of abuſe.

K. LEAR.

P. 583.

Here our learned editor, incapable of diſtinguiſh-ing hiſtory from romance, quotes Geoffrey of Monmouth for " an hiſtorical fact." In a ſubſe-quent page (601) he aſſures us that " *Nero* is intro-duced in the preſent play above 800 years before he was born." He ſhould therefor ſeem to have ſome ſecret method for aſcertaining the æra of perſons that never exiſted, and of events that never hap-pened. It cannot, however, be by means of the *black·art*, as he is certainly *no conjurer*.

P. 587.

Your old kind father, whofe frank heart gave
you all.

Father, brother, rather, he has already obferved,
he fays, were fometimes ufed by Shakıbeare as monofyllables :

Your old kind *fa'r,* whofe frank heart gave
you all.

The folios read :

Your old kind father, whofe frank heart gave all.

The poetical reader will judge which line is moft
likely to have fallen from Shakfpeare.

V O L.   IX.

ROMEO AND JULIET.

P. 66.

Jul. Romeo!
Rom. Madam.

" Thus," fays Mr. Malone, " the original copy
of 1597. In the two fubfequent copies and the folio
we have — My *niece.* What word was intended by
it is difficult," for him, " to fay. The editor of the

fecond folio," he adds, " fubftituted—My *fweet :*"
which, being an emendation equally juft and beautiful, and, by his own admiffion, more " tender"
than what he calls " the original word," he rejects as
an arbitrary fubftitution, " all the alterations in that
copy" being " made at random ;" not excluding
thofe which this candid commentator has elfewhere
thought fit to adopt.

Madam, which is given to Romeo, in the firft
copy, by a mere miftake of the compofitor, evidently belongs to the nurfe, who is fuppofed to call
Juliet from within. Shakfpeare, however, thought
proper to alter the word to *fweet*, and give it to
Romeo; or indeed one of the fpeeches may have
dropped out at the prefs. *Neece* is a palpable mifprint.

P. 100.

Hood my unmann'd blood.

" To hood a hawk, that is to cover its head with
a hood," we are here told, " was an ufual practice,
before the bird was fuffered to fly at its quarry."

If fuch a practice ever prevailed, I conclude it
muft have been in our luminous editors native
country. It will appear a very ftrange doctrine
to the amateurs of this favage amufement, that the
hawk fhould be flown at game which it was not
fuffered to fee. The fact is that they, on this occafion, took the hood *off*.

P. 113.

But thou flew'ft Tybalt; there art thou happy too.

" Thus," he fays, " the firft quarto. In the fub-fequent quartos, and the folio *too* is omitted."

Now, reader, be pleafed to mark the candour, the integrity of this ingenuous critic. The editor of the *fecond folio*, who, he pretends, has been the moft arbitrary, ignorant and capricious of the whole fet, reads exactly with the *firft quarto*. What fay you to this, M. Malone? Is this too an alteration made at random and fuggefted by ignorance and caprice?

P. 123.

When the fun fets the *air* doth drizzle dew.

The reading of fome editions is—the *earth* doth drizzle dew—which our editor fays is philofophically true, and ought to be preferred.

No one I believe ever before heard of the earths *drizzleing dew.* The editor feems to have got his philofophy out of Dr. Hills *Infpector*, which, to be fure, is a very proper fchool for fuch a novice. That Shakfpeare, however, thought it was the *air* and not the *earth* that *drizzled dew* is evident from other paffages.

So in *K. John :*

Before the *dew* of evening *fall.*

Again in *K. Henry VIII.*

His *dews fall* every where.

Again, in the fame play:

The *dews* of *heaven fall* thick in bleffings on
her.

Again, in Hamlet:

Dews of blood *fell.*

I fuppofe we are in thefe places to read *earth*
for *heaven* and *rife* or *rofe* inftead of *fall* or *fell.*

HAMLET.

P. 217.

Lends the tongue vows : thefe blazes, daughter.

Some epithet, he fays, has been omitted in confequence of which the metre is defective. There is
not the fmalleft ground for fuch a fuppofition :
Blazes is a *quadrifyllable.* We may therefor read:

Lends the tongue vows : thefe *bla-a-à-zes,*
daughter.

P. 426.

Of *carnal,* bloody and unnatural acts.

" A *feeble Remarker,*" as this Herculean commentator elegantly obferves, " afks " was the rela-

N

tionſhip between the uſurper and the deceaſed king
a ſecret confined to Horatio?" "No," he anſwers,
"but the *murder* of Hamlet by Claudius was a
ſecret which the young prince had imparted to Horatio alone; and to this it is he *principally*, though
covertly alludes."

And, pray, what is all this to the ſignification of
the word *carnal?* But it is natural enough for a
feeble Remark to produce a *pitiful cavil* from a *half-
informed hypercritic.*

OTHELLO.

P. 445.

——muſt be *belee'd* and calm'd.

"The *lee*-ſide of a ſhip," we are told, "is that
on which the wind blows. To *lee*, or to be *lee'd*
may," therefor "mean, to fall to leeward, or to loſe
the advantage of the wind."

Alexander the great, after liſtening to the laboured
oration of a pedantic philoſopher on the art of war,
obſerved that he had never heard a fool talk ſo learn-
edly. This compliment cannot poſſibly be applyed to
our editor, who always talks like himſelf; pretending
to know every thing and knowing nothing. One
would have thought that every fool knew that the
lee ſide of a ſhip is that—not *on* which, but *from*
which the wind blows. The editor has read in the

newfpapers of a *lee-fhore*, which would be there rightly interpreted, a fhore *on* which the wind blows ; but it is fo termed in reference to the *fhip*, as being a fhore on its *lee fide*. *Belee'd* is a word formed like *becalm'd*, &c. and means, as other perfons have rightly explained it, that Caffio intercepted the wind of favour or preferment.

P. 537.

Keep leets and lawdays.

" The *leet*," our learned editor obferves, " according to Lambard, was a *court* or jurifdiction above the wapentake or hundred, comprehending three or four hundreds. The *jurifdiction* of this court is now in moft places merged in that of the *county court*."

There is, I am perfuaded, fome mifreprefentation as well as fome ignorance in this note. As to the firft charge, he may acquit himfelf of it by producing a paffage in which Lambard has any fuch affertion. Upon the fecond count, Ignorance, he muft be clearly convicted. The *Leet* being a *criminal court* as well as a *court of record* never had, nor poffibly could have, the flighteft connection with the *county court*, which is neither the one nor the other, and confequently cannot have merged in it. You fee, therefor, M. Malone, that your friend Minfhew is not always to be depended upon.

N 2

VOL. X.

TITUS ANDRONICUS.

P. 388.

Was there none elſe in Rome to make a ſtale of.

" The words, *there*, *elſe*, and *of*, are not found in the *old copies*. This *conjectural emendation* was made by the editor of the *ſecond folio*."

Since our critic has elſewhere ſhewn (as he ſays) " that all the alterations in this edition were made at random," and that the editor was entirely ignorant of our authors phraſeology and metre, how comes i ; that his arbitrary innovation of no leſs than three words ſhould have been honoured with a place in our authors text? Becauſe, for once, he has omitted to perceive that Shakſpeare uſed the words *none Rome*, and other words of that kind, as diſſyllables and conſequently the metre " was to his ear perfect."

Was *none* in *Rome* to make a ſtale.

P. 451.

Even from *Hyperion's* riſing in the eaſt.

" The [firſt] folio," ſays Mr. Steevens, " reads *Epton's*; the quarto *Epion's*: to which Mr. Malone, without blufhing, adds, " the correction was made in the fecond folio ;" moft inconfiftently deferting the *only true ancient authentic copies* for the *arbitrary emendation* of an *ignorant* editor in an edition of *no value whatever?*

P. 467.

It is obfervable that our equally modeft and con-fiftent critic thinks it " highly probable" that the fecond fcene of the third act of this play " was added by our author :" an opinion for which he has here attempted to ridicule a much more refpectable cha-racter than himfelf; and one whofe judgment feems, from this inftance, at leaft, to have been altogether upon a par with his own. See the Preface, p. lix.

APPENDIX.

P. 599.

Vol. iv. Tw. N. p. 46. He has obferved, he fays, that *lover* is elfewhere ufed by our poet as a word of one fyllable. So, in *A Midfummer Night's Dream :*

" Tie up my *lover's* tongue ; bring him fi-lently."

Again, in *King Henry VIII.*

" Is held no great good *lover* of the archbi-fhops."

As to the firſt of theſe pretended inſtances, it proves
nothing ; being only (whatever he may ſay to the
contrary) a miſprint for *love's*. And every one but
this ſagacious critic will perceive that the other is to
be pronounced like what it is, a word of two ſylla-
bles :

Is held no great good *lover* of th' archbiſhops.

P. 643.

H. V.
P. 492. His noſe was as ſharp as a *pen*, and
'a babbled of green fields.

On this difficult paſſage our editor had one conjecture which had luckily, it ſeems, eſcaped him
when the play was printing, but he unfortunately
recollected it in time for his appendix. It is that
the word *table* is right, and the corrupted word *and*,
which may have been miſprinted for *in* ; and thus
then the paſſage will mean—" and his note was as
ſharp as a *pen* in a *table* of green fields." A *pen*
may have been uſed for a *pin-fold*, and a table for a
picture. The pointed ſtakes, he adds, of which
pinfolds are ſometimes formed were perhaps in the
poets thoughts.

Riſum teneatis ? If Shakſpeare had had the pointed
ſtakes of a pinfold in his minds eye he would
have mentioned it, for though the *ſtake* may be ſharp,
the *pinfold* is not. But why waſte a moment in the

consideration of such miserable nonsense? Whoever knew the word *pen* used for *pinfold*, or a pinfold placed amidst a parcel of green fields? We have *pens* for *geese*, indeed, and *pens* for *sheep*; but no one ever before heard of the *pen* of an *ass*.

P. 643.

P. 495. " An anonymous writer," we are told, " supposes that by the words—*keep close*, Pistol means *keep within doors*. That this was not the meaning," it seems, " is proved decisively by the words of the quarto."

That this is not the meaning in the quarto may be proved decisively by the words of that edition, but the meaning of the folio is to be ascertained by its own: so that the supposition may be right enough.

Such are the observations which I have had to make upon this most sagacious of editors, and his unparalleled edition. I must not, however, be understood to say that I have paid equal attention to all his absurdities. His pages abound with examples of *profound ignorance, idle conjectures, crude notions, feeble attempts at jocularity, slender criticism, shallow, half-informed, fond, skill-less, tasteless* and *unfounded remarks*, no less, or possibly much more, worthy of contempt and derision than those exposed in the present sheets. They can only, therefor, serve as a hafty or imperfect fketch of what may be done by others; if indeed either Mr. Malone or his edition be intitled to any further notice. It will be eafily feen that, in the courfe of this inveftigation, " I have endeavoured, as much as poffible, to avoid all controverfy ;" and Mr. Malone, I am fure, has too exalted an opinion of his peculiar merits, and too fovereign a contempt for thofe who dare call them in queftion, to permit that the ferenity of his mind fhould fuffer a moments difcompofure by the appearance of an infignificant pamphlet ; well knowing that " of fuch flimzy materials are many of the *hyper-criticifms* compofed to which the labours of the editors and commentators on Shakfpeare have given rife."

THE END.

A

LETTER

TO

The Rev. Dr. FARMER, &c.

A

LETTER

TO THE

Rev. RICHARD FARMER, D.D.

MASTER OF EMANUEL COLLEGE, CAMBRIDGE;

RELATIVE TO THE EDITION OF

SHAKSPEARE,

PUBLISHED IN MDCCXC.

AND SOME LATE CRITICISMS ON THAT WORK.

By EDMOND MALONE, Esq.

Alter rixator de lana sæpe caprina
Propugnat, nugis armatus; scilicet, ut non
Sit mihi prima fides, et vere quod placet, ut non
Acriter elatrem, pretium ætas altera sordet. Hor.

—— QUEM OPINIO PROPRIÆ PERSPICACIÆ, QUA SIBI
VIDETUR ERRORES QUOSDAM ANIMADVERTISSE, DE
STATU MENTIS DETURBAVIT. B. Jonson.

LONDON:

PRINTED FOR G. G. J. AND J. ROBINSON, PATERNOSTER-ROW;
T. PAYNE, AT THE MEUSE-GATE; AND R. FAULDER, IN
BOND STREET.

MDCCXCII.

A

L E T T E R

TO

The Rev. DR. FARMER, &c.

MY DEAR SIR,

THOUGH you have long left the *primroſe path* of poetry and criticiſm, for more grave and important ſtudies, you will, I am confident, very cheerfully ſpend an hour with me in tra-verſing the old Shakſpearian field, where we have ſo often expatiated on " the ever-fruitful ſubject" of our great dramatick poet and his Commentators.

When I firſt undertook to give an edition of his Works, it did not appear to me ſo arduous a taſk as I found it. After devoting ſeveral years to their reviſal and elucidation, I had the honour to preſent my edition to the publick in November, 1790, and immediately afterwards ſet

out

out on a visit to some very dear friends in Ireland, whom I had not seen for a long time. During my stay there, I was not a little pleased to learn from every quarter that my work had not been disapproved of by the publick; and on my return to England last summer was still more highly gratified by your warm, and I fear too partial, approbation of my labours; by that of Mr. Burke, whose mind is of such a grasp as to embrace at once the greatest and the minutest objects, and who, in the midst of his numerous and important avocations, has always found time for the calmer pursuits of philosophy and polite literature; by that of the most amiable and judicious friend whom we and the publick have lately had the irreparable misfortune to lose, Sir Joshua Reynolds; of that excellent critick and profound scholar, Dr. Joseph Warton; and of many others, whose encomiums would stamp a value on any literary performance. When I mention these respected names, let me shelter myself under the example of the great poet who preceded me in this undertaking:

" Well-natured Garth inflam'd with early
 praise,
" And Congreve lov'd, and Swift endur'd
 my lays."

With

With this detail, I am fenfible, the publick has very little concern; nor is it obtruded on them from any idle vanity, but merely as a neceffary introduction to the following pages.

The fubject on which I am now to trouble you, has one very unpleafing circumftance attending it; that I cannot difcufs it without introducing myfelf as a principal figure on the canvas. It is, I truft, unneceffary to affure you, who have known me fo long, that it is the laft fubject which I fhould have *chofen*; it has, as you will fee, been forced upon me. However, though from the nature of the difquifition it is impoffible for me to keep where I wifh to remain, in the back ground, I will promife not to detain you long from much more important and interefting topicks.

Almoft all the copies of my edition having been fold, an anonymous writer, at the end of fifteen months, finding it a fubject of fufficient notoriety to procure fome attention to an invective againft it in the form of a pamphlet, has lately thought fit to iffue one from the prefs, fraught with the ufual materials of hypercriticifm; that is, duly furnifhed with unblufhing cavil, falfe argument, and falfe quotation;

with

with
" ————— captious art,
" And fnip fnap fhort, and interruption fmart,
" And demonftration thin, and thefes thick,
" And major, minor, and conclufion quick."

Our late excellent friend, Dr. Johnfon, ufed
to fay, that an author might be fatisfied with
the publick approbation, when his name was
able to *carry double*. In this refpect therefore
this writer fhould feem to have intended me a
compliment, and as fuch I accept it; though
I have not vanity enough to fuppofe that I can
fuftain fuch a heap of rubbifh as has been raked
up, to furnifh the number of pages neceffary
for the occafion.

I will not ftain my paper by tranfcribing
any part of the vulgar ribaldry with which this
production abounds. Let it reft with the low
focieties among whom it has been picked up,
and in the bookfeller's warehoufe, where,
with other neglected trafh, it will long remain in undifturbed repofe. But as two or
three *facts* have been mentioned, which, however diftorted or difcoloured, have fomething
like the femblance, though nothing of the
reality, of truth, I fhall detain you for a fhort
time, folely with a view of obviating the effect
which is fometimes produced by filent contempt and unrefuted mifreprefentation. Our
inimitable

nimitable poet, who on moſt occaſions is our
beſt inſtructor, you remember, adviſes us, not
to " give advantage

" To ſtubborn criticks, apt, *without a theme*,
" For depravation."

The firſt fact that I ſhall take notice of, is
contained in the following paragraph :

" MR. MALONE, in the year 1780, when publiſhing a *Supplement to Shakſpeare* of plays which
he never wrote *, modeſtly remarked, that

* This SUPPLEMENT contained ſeveral additional comments on the author ; a correct edition of all his poems,
then for the firſt time faithfully printed from the original copies, and illuſtrated with notes ; and ſeven plays which had
been *imputed* to him. Theſe I was ſo far from publiſhing
as Shakſpeare's, that I expreſsly declared in the preface that
of five of them I did not believe a ſingle line to have been
written by him ; and my deciſion has been fully confirmed
by the manuſcripts which I have ſince diſcovered in Dul-
wich College, in which the names of the four authors of
Sir John Oldcaſtle (a play printed in 1600, with Shakſpeare's
name at full length in the title-page,) are luckily preſerved.—
See the late edition of Shakſpeare, Vol. I. P. II. *Emendations
and Additions*, p. 317.—The writer's *meaning*, however, as
honeſt *Sir Hugh Evans* ſays, *was good* ; for from the words—
" A Supplement to Shakſpeare *of plays which he never wrote*,"
the reader would naturally conclude, 1. that this Supplement
contained plays only ; and 2. that the editor was weak
enough to believe them to be the productions of our author,
and to aſcribe to him *what he never wrote.*

' by

(6)

' by a diligent collation of all the old copies
*thitherto** difcovered, and the judicious reftoration
of ancient readings, the text of this author
feemed then finally fettled.' Since that period,
however, he has been labouring ' with unceafing
folicitude,' for the fpace of 'eight years,' to convince the publick that he had, if not directly
afferted the thing which was not, at leaft gone
a little further than was confiftent with the
exact ftate of the cafe. For, if the text had
been already diligently collated with all the old
copies, why fhould he make fuch a parade of
having collated it himfelf? If it had not been
fo collated, why fhould he fay it had ? This fact is
therefore manifeft, upon Mr. Malone's own evidence, that the text of Shakfpeare had never been
collated, whether diligently or not, with all or any
of the old copies, by any perfon before Mr.
Malone."

Twenty fix years have now elapfed fince Mr.
Steevens iffued out propofals for publifh-
ing the plays of Shakfpeare, of which in that
period he has given the publick three editions,
each of them elaborated with his utmoft care
and diligence. The year 1766, in which his
propofals firft came forth, fhould be doubly dear

To this *quaintnefs* a line of Martial may be well applied:
" — male cum recitas, incipit effe tuus."

to every intelligent reader of this poet; not
only as the era when that gentleman firſt. undertook the arduous taſk of illuſtrating his dra-
mas by the contemporary writers, a taſk which
he executed with great ability, but becauſe the
moſt concluſive Eſſay * that ever appeared on
a ſubject of criticiſm, was then written, and
the long-agitated queſtion concerning the learning of Shakſpeare was for ever decided. In
the year 1780, fourteen years after Mr. Steevens's work was firſt undertaken, and two years
after the ſecond edition of it had appeared, I publiſhed a Supplement to that edition in two volumes, in the preface to which is the paragraph above quoted. Having a very high opinion
of the diligence, acuteneſs, and learning of Mr.
Steevens, to whom all the admirers of Shakſpeare have great obligations, I in common
with the reſt of the publick conſidered myſelf
as much indebted to his labours ; and therefore
did not then heſitate to ſay that the text of the
author on which he had been above twelve years
employed, *ſeemed* to be finally ſettled. If I had
uſed a ſtill ſtronger phraſe, ſome allowance might
be made for the partiality of friendſhip, and for
that reſpect which is due from every ſcholar to ac-

* *An Eſſay on the Learning of Shakſpeare,* by the Rev.
Richard Farmer; publiſhed in January, 1767 ; reprinted,
with great additions, in the ſame year.

B 4   knowledged

knowledged abilities and learning. But I claim
no such allowance; for I said only what I strictly
and sincerely thought. Not choosing however
to speak confidently and positively of a matter
concerning which I could not be certain, I used
the words—"*seems* now finally settled." I had not
then undertaken to publish an edition of Shakspeare, nor regularly collated a single play of
that author with the authentick copies. When
my admiration of his innumerable beauties led
me to undertake an edition of his works, I
then thought it my duty to exert every faculty
to make it as perfect as I could; and in order
to ensure a genuine text, to collate word by
word every line of his plays and poems with
the original and authentick copies; a task equally new and arduous. By this laborious process
I obtained ONE THOUSAND SIX HUNDRED AND
FIFTY FOUR EMENDATIONS of the text; that
is, I found that the text of this author, notwithstanding all the well-employed diligence
and care of the late editors in correcting the
errors of former copies, and rejecting the adul-
terations introduced in the second folio and the
subsequent impressions, still remained corrupted
in sixteen hundred and fifty four places, and I
corrected it accordingly; not as that word is
sometimes understood, by capricious innovation, or fanciful conjecture, but by the restoration

tion of the poet's words, as they are found in the only copies of authority.

We are now, however, told, that from this collation but little advantage has been derived ; and, as a *proof* of this affertion, it is ftated, that in collating ONE HUNDRED THOUSAND LINES (for fuch nearly is the number of lines in thefe plays) I have not always been equally attentive ; that in this tedious labour (wonderful to tell!) I have been guilty of *eight* errors !! fo that it appears, that I have only corrected the plays of this author in *one thoufand fix hundred and fifty-four places*, and might have corrected them in *one thoufand fix hundred and fixty-two*. Of thefe eight additional reftorations I fhall very gladly avail myfelf in the quarto edition of this poet's works, which I am now about to put to the prefs * ;

and

---

* While foreign countries can boaft of magnificent impreffions of the works of their celebrated authors, a fplendid edition of the Plays and Poems of our great dramatick poet, with the illuftrations which the various editors and commentators have furnifhed, is yet a *defideratum* in Englifh literature. I had ten years ago fketched out a plan for fuch an edition, and intend immediately to carry a fimilar fcheme into execution. It is almoft unneceffary to add, that the fame gratuitous zeal which induced me to undertake the former edition, will accompany this revifal of it ; and that no diligence

gence

and if from any quarter, however unrefpectable, others fhall be added to that number, they fhall be accepted in like manner; but I do not expect that will be the cafe; as it is probable, if any further difcoveries of the fame kind could have been made, they would have been pointed out. *Dum filent, clamant.*—Dr. Johnfon has juftly obferved, that a difcurfive mind cannot be always kept fteadily fixed on evanefcent truth. I never flattered myfelf fo far as to fuppofe, that in this long woʒk " the indifpofed and fickly fit" fhould not fometimes render me unequal to the tafk; that what happens to all mankind, occafional languor and temporary inability, fhould not affect me like other mortals: I refolved, however, to make the beft exertions in my power; and fometimes flattered myfelf that by this procefs, which had never before been attempted, and a long acquaintance with the writers of Shakfpeare's age, I fhould be able to improve on all the former editions of this author; but in the moment of the moft fanguine hope I could not fuppofe that in this col-

gence or care of mine fhall be wanting to render this new edition of my work, which is to be ornamented with engravings, and to be printed in fifteen volumes, royal quarto, worthy of our greateft Englifh poet.—The firft two volumes are intended to be publifhed next year.

lation

lation my vigilance fhould have been over-
watched only in eight inftances; nor, without fo
decifive a proof as the malignant induftry of a
petty adverfary has furnifhed, could I have
believed it. I fay *eight* inftances; for though
thirteen over-fights have been enumerated,
five of them *have no foundation in truth.*

1. The firft of thefe is in *The Two Gentlemen
of Verona,* Vol. I. p. 154.

Speed. Item, fhe can *few.*

Launce. That's as much as to fay, can fhe
fo?

" *Both* the folios," fays this redoubted critick, " read—*fow,* which is manifeftly requifite. Probably, however, the editor may
fuppofe *few* and *fo* to have the fame pronunciation."

With the fecond folio, here cited, or any other
corrupted copy of our author, I have no concern.
The firft and *only* authentick copy of this play
printed in folio, in 1623, (for there is no quarto,)
reads, if letters are to be enumerated, not *fow,* but
fowe. When a quibble is intended, the word in the
old copy is often intentionally mifpelt, in order
to

to mark it more plainly to the reader. In the
prefent inftance, however, this may not have been
the cafe, for the word *few* was varioufly fpelt
in Shakfpeare's time, and Milton writes it,
though improperly, *fow*. Throughout my edition, as is mentioned in my preface, I have not
adhered to ancient fpelling, but adopted that
which is now generally ufed, and which I confidered as juft. I have done fo in this inftance.
With refpect to the fimilarity of found between
few and *fo*, there can be no doubt, from the paffage before us, but that the two words were
pronounced alike in Shakfpeare's days, as they
are at prefent by all who do not deviate from re-
ceived modes from affectation or ignorance.

2. Vol. II. p. 71. *Meafure for Meafure.*

" Let me hear you fpeak *further*." " Both
editions — *farther*, a word entirely different from
further, though too frequently confounded with
it by ignorant perfons."

Here is a queftion merely of propriety in
fpelling, and whenever I have any doubts on
that fubject I fhall take counfel from fome other
preceptor than this critick. In the authentick
copy of 1623, the word is very frequently
fpelt

ſpelt *farther*, for which, on the ground already mentioned, I have given *further*, becauſe that appears to me to be the true mode of ſpelling this word; and Dr. Johnſon, whoſe authority is ſomewhat higher than this anonymous wri-ter's, was of this opinion*. The two words were undoubtedly uſed indiſcriminately by Shakſpeare, who certainly did not give himſelf much concern about grammatical diſquiſi-tions.

3. The third ſuppoſed error, for which I am not anſwerable as an overſight in collating the old copies, is in Vol. II. p. 151. *The Comedy of Errors.*

" If it be, ſir, pray eat none of it."

It is a mere error of the preſs. The pro-noun *I* (I pray, eat none of it,) I find, on looking into my papers, was inadvertently omitted by the compoſitor at the preſs, as the metre of the line ſhews.

4. Vol. II. p. 190. *Ibidem.*

" And much different from the man he was."

" The folios (we are told) read—And much, *much* different."

* See his *Dict.* in v. *further.*

The

(14)

The single remark here neceſſary to be made is, that *the fact is not ſo*. The only authentick copy of this play, the folio of 1623, which is now before me, exhibits the line as I have printed it.

5. Vol. II. p. 477. *A Midſummer-Night's Dream.*

" Through the foreſt have I gone,
" But Athenian *found* I none."

" *All* the old editions (we are again inſtructed) read—*find*."

Here we have another inſtance of dogmatical and preſumptuous ignorance ; and the ſame ſhort anſwer will ſerve. *The fact is not ſo.* The copy of *A Midſummer-Night's Dream*, printed by Fiſher, which is in ſome places preferable to that printed by Roberts, which laſt appears to have been followed in the folio, reads— " *found* I none," as I have printed the line.

The *eight* reſtorations which I am now enabled to add to thoſe I have already made in the text, are theſe : In Vol. I. p. 80, I have inadvertently followed former editors in printing " if *thou* be pleas'd," for— " if *you* be pleas'd ;" in p. 140 of the ſame volume, " *more* precious," for— " *moſt* precious ;" in p. 155, " *I cannot* help,"
for

for—"*cannot I* help;" in p. 174, "*this* paper,"
" for *his* paper;" in Vol. II. p. 70, *fhould*, for
fhall; in p. 143, *difpos'd*, for *beftow'd*; in
p. 157, " Ay, let none enter," for—" Ay, *and*
let none enter;" and in p. 190, *therefore*, for
thereof.

It is not an incurious fpeculation to confider
how many errors the writer to whom I am indebted for the above lift, would have been
guilty of in collating and printing one hundred
thoufand lines. He tells us himfelf that fome
remarks which he publifhed a few years ago,
" have been reprefented as the moft incorrect
publication that ever appeared, and that, from
the lift of *errata* in the book itfelf, and the additional one given in another pamphlet, the
charge does not feem to be without foundation."
We have feen that in collating *thirteen* paffages
he has committed, if not *three*, certainly *two*
errors ; if therefore he had undertaken to collate
one hundred thoufand lines, his inaccuracies
according to the moft moderate calculation
would only have amounted to about FIFTEEN
THOUSAND.

The next high crime and mifdemeanor with
which the late editor of Shakfpeare is charged,
is,

is, that in his preface he has *proved* the editor
of the second folio, printed in 1632, to have
been entirely ignorant of Shakfpeare's phrafeology and metre, and the book itfelf *of no* AU-
THORITY *whatfoever* ; yet moft ftrangely and inconfiftently he has adopted fome emendations of
the text from that corrupted copy. To the firft
part of this charge I plead guilty, but am at a
lofs to know under what penal ftatute it fhould
be claffed. To this minute critic indeed,
who alfo publifhed in 1783 fome remarks on
Mr. Steevens's edition of Shakfpeare, (in which
that gentleman, Dr. Johnfon, and others, were
treated with juft as much decency and refpect,
as our late ingenious and learned friend Mr.
Warton had been in another forgotten pamphlet,) to him it was a very ferious grievance ;
for he appears to have fet up for a hypercritick
on Mr. Steevens, without a fingle quarto copy
of our author's plays, and, I fufpect, without being
poffeffed of the only authentick folio edition. If
that was the cafe, to depreciate the vitiated folio
on which he was generally obliged to depend,
was to rob him of the only tool with which he
could carry on his trade, and to place him in the
ftate in which poor Parfon Adams would have
found himfelf, if his hoft had convinced him that
his folitary half-guinea was a counterfeit.

With

With refpect to the other part of the charge, it is certainly true that while almoft every page of the fecond folio is disfigured by printer's blunders, and arbitrary and capricious deviations from the original copy, the editor of that book has in a few places corrected fuch manifeft errors of the prefs in the elder copy, as could not efcape a perfon of the moft ordinary capacity, who had been but one month converfant with a printing-houfe. Of thefe corrections, fuch as they are, (to the knowledge of which the objector was led by my own notes,) a pompous lift has been made from the late edition, for the purpofe of fhewing an inconfiftency in the editor: but in the courfe which I have followed, when the matter is truly ftated and examined, the fmalleft inconfiftency will not be found.

To afcertain whether the fecond complete edition of our author's plays was authentick, which had never been attempted before, was, in forming the text of thofe plays, of the higheft confequence. Hence it was that I employed a good deal of labour on that point, as may be feen by turning to my preface, where the examination of that queftion takes up no lefs than twenty-three pages *; and I may ven-

* Pref. pp. xix—xlii.

C

ture

ture to fay, without any fear of being refuted, that I have *proved*, not by dogmatical affertion, but by a minute enumeration of particular paffages, that book to be of no *authority* whatfoever. How fo wild a notion as that it was of any authority, fhould ever have been entertained by any one but the writer whofe mifreprefentations I am now expofing, is perfectly unaccountable. The fecond edition of a printed book can only derive authority from its being printed with the author's laft corrections, or from fome more correct manufcript of his work than that from which the firft edition was printed. From whence fhould the authority of the fecond folio be derived? We know that Shakfpeare did not correct his manufcripts for the prefs, even for the firft edition which was publifhed in 1623:—where then were the corrections which were made in the fecond, found? Can it be believed, that the printer or editor, who did not, as I have proved incontrovertibly, examine one of the quarto printed plays*, which were then common in every hand, fhould have hunted after the manufcripts from which the firft folio was in fome cafes

* Pref. to the late edition of Shakfpeare, p. xxvii, note 4.

printed,

printed, and which it is highly probable were
deftroyed at the prefs; or that any diligence
fhould at the end of nine years have recovered
their foiled and mutilated fragments? Such a
fuppofition is as wild and chimerical, as many
of that editor's arbitrary interpolations. This
fancy fhould feem to have originated from its
having been thrown out in fome modern publication, the title of which I have forgotten, that
Heminge and Condell, the editors of the firft
folio, were *probably* likewife editors of the fecond, which appeared in 1632; an affertion
which, before the two books had been minutely
examined and compared, and before the time
of their refpective deaths had been afcertained,
might pafs current enough; but unluckily for
this theory, after a long fearch in the Preroga-
tive Office, I difcovered the wills of both thefe
actors, and have fhewn that Condell died in
1627, and Heminge in the year 1630*.—
On this fubject, however, we are not obliged
to have recourfe to inferences from dates, or to
conjecture, in order to prove that all the corrections, emendations, or interpolations of that
copy (by whatever name they may be called)
were arbitrary and capricious. The nume-

*Hiftorical Account of the Englifh ftage, pp. 190. 199,

rous

rous proofs which I collected for this purpose, were given *ex abundanti*. If instead of shewing that the editor, not knowing that the double comparative was the common phraseology of Shakspeare's time, had substituted for it a more grammatical form, giving us *more safe*, *more worthy* and *more rich*, for *more safer*, *more worthier* and *more richer*; that he did not know that the double negative was the common and authorized language of that age *; that when the beginning of a line in the elder copy was accidentally omitted at the press, instead of attempting to cure the defect in the right place, he added some words at the end of the line, and by his addition made the passage nonsense †; that he was utterly ignorant of his author's elliptical language, as well as of his metre;—if instead of all these proofs and many others to the same point, I had produced only one of them, it would have been sufficient for my purpose, and the old adage—*ex uno disce omnes* would have supplied the rest.

* As in *The Comedy of Errors*, Act III. sc. ii.
    " *Nor* to her bed *no* homage do I owe ;"
instead of which we have in the second folio,
    " Nor to her bed *a* homage do I owe."

† Pref. to the late edit. p. xxxi.

Notwith-

Notwithftanding, however, all that I have now ftated, you know there are fome men in the world, who will not relinquifh their old *mumpfimus*; who when once they have taken up a particular notion, adhere to it with unconquerable pertinacity, and cannot be argued out of it : With fuch men, neither the decifive circumftance I have juft now mentioned, (the death of our poet's friends, Heminge and Condell, before the end of 1630,) nor the unanfwerable proofs which I have accumulated of the ignorance and temerity of the editor of the fecond folio, will have the fmalleft weight, or at all depreciate its credit: and if they fhould ever be allowed to fcribble in the margin of Shakfpeare, notwithftanding thefe accumulated proofs we fhould without doubt be reminded, whenever occafion offered, that " Such is the reading of that moft excellent and invaluable book the fecond folio edition of our author's plays; a reading which Mr. M. has not been afhamed to own that he has adopted, though he has exprefsly denied the authenticity of the book".

And now let me add a word or two on the fubject of inconfiftency. Though I proved this book of no *authority* whatfoever, does it therefore follow that I was precluded from

adopting

adopting the few emendations of manifeſt errors
of the preſs, which, amidſt ſome thouſand innovations and corruptions, were made by the
editor; and which, if they had not been made
by him, would unqueſtionably have been made
by ſome other perſon? The plan which I
adopted for my edition, as far as relates to the
text, was very ſimple. I began by aſcertaining
what were the authentick copies. I then formed
my text upon thoſe copies; from which (with
the exception mentioned in my preface) I never
knowingly deviated without apprizing the reader by a note. All emendations therefore
which were admitted, from whatever quarter
taken, are regularly aſcribed to him by whom
they were made; a piece of juſtice which had
not been done in former editions : and neither
the caprice of an editor or commentator, or his
general inability for his taſk, prevented me from
adopting corrections ſuggeſted by him, if they
were manifeſtly right. Thus, ſome emendations have been taken even from Pope and
Hanmer, as well as from the editor of the ſecond folio; though all theſe editors have with
almoſt equal licentiouſneſs corrupted the author's text; but they are adopted, not becauſe
their books are of any *authority*, but becauſe
the emendations themſelves are evidently juſt;
for

for the editor of the second folio, as soon as his book is proved not to be authentick, can rank only by the side of any other conjecturer, commentator, or verbal critick. And on the same ground, if the most obscure and contemptible pamphleteer should suggest a happy correction of any desperate passage, manifestly corrupt, to the propriety and rectitude of which every intelligent reader must at once assent, it would have a claim to attention, however little respect should be due to the quarter from whence it came. With how much caution however I have proceeded in this respect, my book will shew.

If the second folio had been of any *authority*, then all the capricious innovations of that copy (in which description I do not include the innumerable errors of the press) must have been adopted ; but being once proved not to be authentick, then in the case of a passage undoubtedly corrupt in the original and authentick copies, we are at liberty to admit an emendation suggested by any later editor or commentator, if a neater and more plausible correction than that furnished by the second folio ; and this I have done more than once.

On

On comparing two of the quarto editions of
King Richard III. I found that there were in
the latter no lefs than twenty-fix errors of omiffion; and indeed errors of omiffion are, I
believe, more frequent than almoft any other
in the ancient copies of this author. I have
proved in various inftances, that when a
word was omitted or corrupted in the firft folio,
the editor of the fecond either left the paffage
as he found it, or cured the defect at random,
and according to his fancy, in thofe plays of
which we have quarto copies, where the true
word, which in fact was omitted or corrupted,
may be found.* There cannot therefore be the
fmalleft doubt that all the emendations made by
this editor in the other plays alfo, of which
there are no quarto copies, were merely conjectural. Being fuch, they ftand precifely on
the fame ground with the emendations fuggefted by any later editor or commentator; and
as they are often very injudicious in confequence of the editor's extreme ignorance of
Shakfpeare's phrafeology and metre, they ftand
frequently on a worfe ground, and have a lefs
title to be adopted.

* Pref. to the late edition, pp. xiv. xv. xxvii. n. 4;
xxx. xxxi.

The

(25)

The few corrections which have been taken from that copy, on the principle juſt now mentioned,* have been pompouſly diſplayed ;
a liſt

---

* Such as, in *The Tempeſt*,

" —— ſuch *iſlanders*,"
inſtead of the erroneous reading of the authentick copy,—
" ſuch *iſland*s."

In *The Two Gentlemen of Verona*,
" —— and I *a* ſheep."
for   " —— and I *ſheep*."

Ibidem. "—— you have *teſtern'd* me."
for   "   —— you have *ceſtern'd* me."

In *Meaſure for Meaſure*,
" The *princely* Angelo."
for   " The *prenzie* Angelo."

Ibid.   " —— ache, *penury*, and impriſonment."
for   "   —— ache, *perjury*, and impriſonment."

Ibid.   " —— was affianced to her *by* oath,
for   "   —— was affianced *to her oath*.

In *The Comedy of Errors*,
" Gave *helpful* welcome ——."
for   " Gave *healthful* welcome ——."

Ibid.   " And as a *bed* I'll take thee, and there lie."
inſtead of " And as a *bud*, &c."

Ibid.

a lift of them having been collected from my
own volumes, without the aid of which it does
not

Ibid. " Mafter, if *you* do —."
inftead of " Mafter, *if do* —."

In *As you like it,*

" —— that which had too *much.*"
for " —— that which had too *muft.*"

Ibid. " Let me *be* better acquainted with thee,
for " Let me better acquainted with thee.

In *The Taming of the Shrew,*
" Were fhe as rough —."
for " Were fhe *is* as rough —."

Ibid. " As much news as *thou wilt.*"
for " As much news as *wilt thou.*"

Ibid. " Whither away, and *where* is thy abode."
for " Whither away, and *whither* is thy abode."

In *All's well that ends well,*
" —— captious and *intenible* fieve—
for " —— captious and *intemible* fieve."

In *Twelfth Night,*
" Let thy tongue *tang* with arguments of ftate.
for " Let thy tongue *langer,* &c.

In *Macbeth,*
" —— before *thy* here-approach."
for " —— before *they* here approach.

In

not appear that it could have been made, at leaſt it never was made before the late edition was publiſhed.

In *King John,*

"——— to hurt his maſter, no *man* elſe."
inſtead of " ——— to hurt his maſter, no *mans* elſe."

In *King Henry VIII.*

" Good man, thoſe joyful tears ſhew thy true heart."
inſtead of " Good man, thoſe joyful tears ſhew thy true hearts."

A few more emendations of nearly the ſame kind might be added, which together with the above are regularly noticed in the late edition. The interpolations, omiſſions, and corruptions of every kind in the ſecond folio, (of which the fiftieth part has not been noticed) amount, on the other hand, *to ſeveral thouſands.*

I may add, that of the very few emendations ſomewhat leſs obvious than the above, which I have admitted, and which do not, I think, amount to ſix, I find every day ſome reaſon to doubt. Juſt as my edition was iſſuing from the preſs, I found that with the other modern editors I had improperly adopted a word which had been unneceſſarily ſupplied by this editor, from his not attending to Shakſpeare's elliptical language. The paſſage is in *A Midſummer-Night's Dream*, Act I. ſc. i.

" Ere I will yield my virgin patent up
" Unto his lordſhip, whoſe unwiſhed yoke
" My ſoul conſents not to give ſovereignty."

i. e.

publifhed. By turning over the pages of my work, as I have conftantly noticed from whence every emendation was taken, this lift was eafily formed; but it has been exhibited with that inaccuracy which might have been expected; for in *The Merchant of Venice*, Act II. fc. iii. I am reprefented as having adopted a corrupt reading found in the fecond folio, (" If a chriftian *did* not play the knave, and get thee," &c.) though I have exprefsly written a note to fhew that this reading was the offspring of ignorance in the

---

i. e. to give fovereignty *to*. See APPEND. to the late edition, p. 577. Here the fecond folio reads—*to* whofe *unwifh'd* yoke, &c. and we are told it is a moft valuable correction.—So I have incautioufly, with the other modern editors, accepted, from the fame book, "*heady* murder," in *K. Henry V.* inftead of "*headly* murder," the corrupt reading of the old copy; but the true reading is undoubtedly—*deadly* murder. So, in *Macbeth*:

" With twenty *mortal murders* on their crowns."

And in *Titus Andronicus* a word which has been fupplied by the fame editor, and too haftily accepted, has this moment caught my eye:

" Was there none elfe in Rome to make a ftale *of*—."

Of, which is not found in the old copy, was introdnced from the fame inadvertence which led to the corruption of the paffage above quoted from *A Midfummer-Night's Dream*. See late edit. Vol. VII. p. 128, n. 8; Vol. VIII. p. 472, n. 3; and Vol. IX. p. 469, n. 3.

editor

editor of that book; in *K. John*, Act II. sc. ii. I am reprefented as having adopted a corrupt reading introduced by the fame editor, —" *run on*," inftead of the authentick reading—*roam* on ; in a paffage in *King Henry V*. Act III. sc. i. I am untruly reprefented as reading with the fame copy,—" You *nobleft* Englifh ;" and ftill *further*, (fave reverence, as our author fays, of the word,) to fhew the amazing acutenefs and unerring accuracy of this hypercritick, the paffage is ftated as being in the Firft Part of *King Henry IV*. as another paffage which is quoted from *Meafure for Meafure*, is to be found in *The Comedy of Errors*.

As a few trifling emendations made by the ignorant editor of the fecond folio, have been adopted, fo on the principle already ftated the very few obfervations of this Remarker that were entitled to any notice, have been admitted into the late edition. Thefe adopted remarks are to be found, fays their author, " in Vol. II. 11, 256, 491, 507 ; III. 27, 77, 316, 394 ; IV. 497, 504; VI. 146, 273; V. 459; [*which is* correctly *placed after Vol. VI.*] VIII. 634." And here we have another fpecimen of this Remarker's extraordinary accuracy; for lo ! neither in p. 256 of Vol. II. nor in p. 316 of Vol.

Vol. III. is there any thing of his; and in p. 27 of Vol. III. I am so far from adopting his comment, that I have maintained a position directly subversive of it.

I shall now, my dear Sir, trouble you with a very few more words.—In *The Two Gentlemen of Verona*, p. 120, I have inserted two notes of my late most respectable friend Mr. Tyrrwhitt, in which he proves that Shakspeare sometimes takes a liberty in extending certain words to complete the measure.* Thus, in *The Comedy of Errors,*

" These are the parents to these *children*."

" where, (says he,) some editors, being unnecessarily alarmed for the metre, have endeavoured to help it by a word of their own,—

" These *plainly* are the parents to these children."

" So, (he adds,) *country* is made a trisyllable.
        T. N. Act. I. sc. ij.
" The like of him. Know'st thou this *country ?*"
        Remembrance, quadrisyllable.
        T. N. Act. I. sc. i.
" And lasting in her sad *remembrance*."

* Mr. Upton had made the same remark. See his *Critical Observations on Shakspeare*, 2d edit. p. 372.

Angry,

Angry, trifyllable.

Timon, Act III. fc. v.

" But who is man, that is not *angry*."

Henry, trifyllable.

Rich. III. Act. II. fc. iii.

" So ftood the ftate when *Henry* the Sixth—"

2 Henry VI. Act. II. fc. ii.

" Crown'd by the name of *Henry* the Fourth."

And fo in many other paffages.

Monftrous, trifyllable.

Macb. Act. IV. fc. vi.

" Who cannot want the thought how *monftrous*—"

Othello, Act. II. fc. iii.

" 'Tis *monftrous*.   Iago, who began it ?"

England, trifyllable.

Rich. II. Act. IV. fc. i.

" Than Bolingbroke return to *England*."

Nobler, trifyllable.

Coriol. Act. III. fc. ii.

" You do the *nobler*.   *Cor*. I mufe my mother—."

It would be quite unneceffary to add that Shakf-peare intended that the words *children, country, monftrous*, fhould in thefe places be pronounced *childeren, countery, monfterous*, if the oppugner of this doctrine had not had the folly to reprefent fuch a notion as chimerical and abfurd ; imagining him-felf (as it fhould feem) fupremely comical, when

6   he

he exhibits words of this kind at full length,—
*Engle-and, noble-er, wrangle-ing, fwor-en, a-rums,
bow-ers,* &c. Had he been at all acquainted
with our elder poets, he would have known
that this pronunciation was fo common, that,
words formerly having been frequently fpelt
by the ear, we often find thefe words written
as Shakfpeare ufed them ; *fower, bower, fier,* &c.

The inftances given above are but a few of
thofe which Mr. Tyrwhitt has collected, to
prove a pofition which is incontrovertible. He
might have produced many more. Thus, in
The Two Gentlemen of Verona, Act. II. fc. iv.

" And that hath *dazzled* my reafon's light ;—"

where the ignorant editor of the fecond folio,
not perceiving that *dazzled* was ufed as a trifyllable, (*dazzle-ed*) has departed from the original
copy, and reads—

" And that hath dazzled *fo* my reafon's light."

Again, in *Coriolanus,* Act. I. fc. ix.

" As you have been ; that's for my *country.*"

And had he not chofen to confine himfelf to
words in which *l,* or *r,* is fubjoined to another
confonant, the following inftances of words ex-
tended for the fake of the metre, might have
been added :

In

In *The Comedy of Errors*, Act. v. fc. i.

" This week he hath been heavy, *four*, fad."

(where in the original copy we find the word
four written as Shakſpeare intended it to be
pronounced,—*ſower* :) and in the ſame play,

" I'll meet you at that place ſome *hour*, hence."

for which in the ſecond folio we have

" I'll meet you at that place ſome hour, *fir*,
hence."

Again, in *K. John*, Act. I. fc. i.

" Kneel thou down, Philip, but riſe *more* great."

Again, in *All's Well that Ends Well*, Act. II.
fc. iii.

" And is not like the *fire*. Honours thrive—".

In all theſe caſes, this hypercritick thinks he
has completely overturned the doctrine contended for, by writing the words at full length,
—*dazzle-ed, counte-ry, ſou-er, ſi-er,* &c. a ſpe-
cies of confutation entirely new. Chauceriz-
ing *more,* and exhibiting it thus,—*mo-ré,* he
ſeems to think extremely humorous. The old
Engliſh name, *Gore,* and the ſurname of a noble family, *Gower,* might have taught him
D   better.

better. *More* and *pour* as easily become *mo-er*
and *pow-er*, as *sour* and *hour* become *sow-er* and
how-er; and *arm*, by a vulgar provincial pronunciation not yet wholly disused becomes
a-rum, as easily as *alarm* is converted into *ala-
rum*; two words that undoubtedly had the
same etymology.—But of these verbal dis-
quisitions enough.

Let us now examine the complaint to which
these notes of Mr. Tyrwhitt's have given birth.
" The editor" [i. e. Mr. M.] we are told, " has
inserted both Mr. Tyrwhitt's notes, without
taking notice of the conclusive reply already
made to the latter." This reply, I must inform you, appears to have been made by this
sagacious remarker himself. *Hinc illæ lacrymæ.*
—But how stands the fact? The comedy of
The Two Gentlemen of Verona was printed in the
year 1786. It should seem therefore not to
have been a crime of very great magnitude
not to have subjoined to Mr. Tyrwhitt's note
a reply to it which was made two years afterwards, viz. in 1788. It might however, we
shall perhaps be told, have been inserted in
the Appendix. But unluckily to this there was
an unsurmountable objection; which was, that
the editor had originally resolved not to encum-

6   ber

ber his page with any uſeleſs comment, and
the *concluſive* reply in queſtion appeared to
him unworthy of notice.

Mr. Tyrwhitt's remark, which I have in part
recited, makes it unneceſſary for me to take
any further notice of the unfounded obſervations
that have been made relative to the licence
which Shakſpeare has occaſionally taken in his
metre. For that licence, which it ſhould be
remembered he has taken in common with his
contemporaries, he alone is anſwerable. If an
editor in exhibiting his works has religiouſly
adhered to the original and authentick copies,
admitting with the greateſt caution occaſional
corrections of manifeſt errors, he has done his
duty, as far as concerns the text; and need
give himſelf little concern about the illiberal cen-
ſures of thoſe who, like the preſent hypercritick,
from ignorance of the poet's metre arraign his
editor, for not having in various inſtances " *endeavoured to help it by a word of his own,*" or
by that which would have been equally improper, an interpolation of Pope or Hanmer, or
the editor of the ſecond folio.

The anonymous writer, who has occaſioned
my preſent addreſs to you, ſeems to think that
he

he has an exclufive privilege to all the nonfenfe
to which the commentaries produced by the
late editors of Shakfpeare have given rife.   On
this ground, a remark in anfwer to one of Dr.
Johnfon's in the firft act of *Troilus and Cref-
fida*, having been flightly noticed in the late
edition, this monopolizer will have it that *he*
muft have been meant; and no fuch remark
being in fact found in his book, with his wonted
decorum he charges the editor with *forgery*.
But ftrange as it may appear, moft true it is,
that there are others now living capable of
writing remarks on Shakfpeare and his editors,
befide himfelf, though not with fuch a total
difregard of decency; and that the obfervation
in queftion appeared among fome REMARKS
on Mr. Steevens's edition, which were publifhed in a mifcellaneous volume, in 1785.

One other paffage only of this *elegant*
and *modeft* performance remains to be noticed.
In the firft volume of the late edition of Shakfpeare I have mentioned that a pamphlet,
which is now avowed by this writer as his
production, was fuppreffed after its original publication, from *modefty* as it fhould feem; and
that afterwards it was once more given to the
world by its author. *Nothing*, fays the fond
parent

parent, *can be more incorrect than this statement. The truth is, that after a few copies had got abroad, the further sale was delayed, for special purposes, for a week, at the end of which the publication was continued.*—Such, I think, is the substance of this *Quip,* for so this writer chooses to denominate some of his shrewd and sagacious remarks, though he does not deal much either in *cranks* or *wanton wiles.* The difference between being *suppressed for a certain time,* and *the sale being delayed, after the original publication, for a week,* is not very easily discovered. The *modesty,* however, ascribed to the author, it must be owned, he utterly disavows.—The grievance stated on this occasion must immediately remind you of that complained of by the well-known Edmund Curl, who said Mr. Pope had treated him very unfairly in telling the publick that he had been toss'd in a *blanket,* when all the world knew that he had only been toss'd in a *rug.*

Though from a very careful perusal of many contemporary writers, I was enabled to make very large additions to the former comments on our author, and took at least as much pains in illustrating his obscurities as in ascertaining his text, you will observe that
I have

(38)

I have not taken notice of any remarks that have been made on the commentaries which I had the honour of fubmiting to the publick in my late edition. While I was employed in preparing them for the prefs, I gave the various fubjects treated of, the strictest attention. They are before the publick, and by its judgment they muft ftand or fall. I fhall not enter into any difcuffion or controverfy with " occafional cricks" or " cricks by profeffion," in order to fupport them.—It is curious that what Dr. Warburton faid near fifty years ago, fhould be ftill true of the *greater part* of the criticifms to which the labours of his fucceffors have given rife : "—as to all thofe things which have been publifhed under the titles of *Effays, Remarks, Obfervations, &c. on Shakfpeare*,"—they " are abfolutely below a ferious notice. *"

I have many apologies to make for having taken up fo much of your time, and will now releafe you. I cannot, however, conclude, without noticing one other charge brought againft the late editor of Shakfpeare, which is

* Mr. Tyrwhitt's *Obfervations* publifhed in 1766, and Mr. Mafon's *Comments* in 1785, are an exception.

perfectly

perfectly novel. " The reciprocal good opinion" (we are told) "which the publick and Mr. MALONE appear to entertain of each other, does both parties infinite honour." It is, I believe, the first time that the good opinion of the publick has ever been stated as a matter of reproach to him who has had the good fortune to obtain it. If by my humble labours I had any title to suppose the publick had been pleased and benefited, I should consider myself as having obtained the best reward which it has to bestow, or the sons of literature ought to aspire to.—To have merited publick approbation, must to an ingenuous mind ever afford a pleasure which the cavils of criticism cannot diminish; and which nothing can so much augment as the disapprobation of the ignorant, the envious, the petulant, and the vain.

I am, my dear Sir,

Your very affectionate friend,

And humble servant,

EDMOND MALONE.

QUEEN-ANNE-STREET, EAST,
April 23, 1792.

EIGHTEENTH CENTURY SHAKESPEARE

During the one hundred and seven years covered by this series, the reputation of William Shakespeare as poet and dramatist rose from a controversial and highly qualified acceptance by post-Restoration critics and "improvers" to the almost idolatrous admiration of the early Romantics and their immediate precursors. Imposing its own standards and interpretations upon Shakespeare, the Eighteenth Century scrutinized his work in various lights. Certain qualities of the plays were isolated and discussed by a parade of learned, cantankerous, and above all self-assured commentators.

Thirty-five of the most important and representative books and pamphlets are here presented in twenty-six volumes; many of the works, through the very fact of their limited circulation have become extremely scarce, and when obtainable, expensive and fragile. The series will be useful not only for the student of Shakespeare's reputation in the period, but for all those interested in eighteenth century taste, taste-making, scholarship, and theatre. Within the series we may follow the arguments and counter-arguments as they appeared to contemporary playgoers and readers, and the shifting critical emphases characteristic of the whole era.

In an effort to provide responsible texts of these works, strict editorial principles have been established and followed. All relevant editions have been compared, the best selected, and the reasons for the choice given. Furthermore, at least one other copy, frequently three or more, have been collated with the copy actually reproduced, and the collations recorded. In cases where variants or cancels exist, every attempt has been made to provide both earlier and later or indifferently varying texts, as appendices. Each volume is preceded by a short preface discussing the text, the publication history, and, when necessary, critical and biographical considerations not readily available.

1. 1692 **Thomas Rymer**
A Short View of Tragedy (1693)
xvi, 184p.   75s.

2. 1693 **John Dennis**
The Impartial Critick: or, some observations upon a late
book, entitled, A Short View of Tragedy, written by
Mr. Rymer, and dedicated to the Right Honourable Charles
Earl of Dorset, etc. (1693)
xvi, 52p.

  1712 **John Dennis**
An Essay on the Genius and Writings of Shakespear: with
some Letters of Criticism to the Spectator (1712)
xxii, 68p.   70s.

3. 1694 **Charles Gildon [ed.]**
Miscellaneous Letters and Essays, on Several Subjects. Philo-
sophical, Moral, Historical, Critical, Amorous, etc. in Prose
and Verse (1694)
xvi, 132p.   55s.

4. 1710 **Charles Gildon**
The Life of Mr. Thomas Betterton, the late Eminent Trage-
dian. Wherein The Action and Utterance of the Stage, Bar,
and Pulpit, are distinctly consider'd . . . To which is added,
The Amorous Widow, or the Wanton Wife . . . Written by
Mr. Betterton. Now first printed from the Original Copy
(1710)
xvi, 176, 87p.   84s.

5. 1726 **Lewis Theobald**
Shakespeare restored: or, A Specimen of the Many Errors,
As well Committed, as Unamended, by Mr. Pope in his Late
Edition of this Poet (1726)
xiii, 194p. 4°   £5 5s.

6. 1747 **William Guthrie**
An Essay upon English Tragedy with Remarks upon the
Abbe de Blanc's Observations on the English Stage (?1747)
34p.

  1749 **John Holt**
An Attempte to Rescue that Aunciente, English Poet, and

Play-wrighte, Maister Williaume Shakespere, from the Maney Errours, faulsely charged on him, by Certaine New-fangled Wittes and to let him speak for Himself, as right well he wotteth, when Freede from the many Careless Mistakeings, of the Heedless first Imprinters, of his Workes (1749)
94p.   55s.

7. 1748 **Thomas Edwards**
The Canons of Criticism and Glossary. Being a Supplement to Mr. Warburton's Edition of Shakespear. Collected from the Notes in that celebrated Work, and proper to be bound up with it. To which are added, The Trial of the Letter Y alias Y; and Sonnets (Seventh Edition, with Additions 1765)
368p.   £5 5s.

8. 1748 **Peter Whalley**
An Enquiry into the Learning of Shakespeare (1748)
84p.
    1767 **Richard Farmer**
As Essay on the Learning of Shakespeare . . . the Second Edition, with Large Additions (1767)
viii, 96p.   70s.

9. 1752 **William Dodd**
The Beauties of Shakespeare: Regularly selected from each Play, With a General Index, Digesting them under Proper Heads. Illustrated with Explanatory Notes and Similar Passages from Ancient and Modern Authors (1752)
2v., xxiv, 264; iv, 258p.   £10 10s.

10. 1753 **Charlotte Ramsay Lennox**
Shakespear Illustrated . . . with Critical Remarks (1753-4)
3v., xiv, 292; iv, 276; iv, 312p.   £15

11. 1765 **William Kenrick**
A Review of Doctor Johnson's New Edition of Shakespeare: In which the Ignorance, or Inattention of That Editor is exposed, and the Poet Defended from the Persecution of his Commentators (1765)
xvi, 136p.
    1766 **Thomas Tyrwhitt**
Observations and Conjectures upon some Passages of

Shakespeare (1766)
ii, 56p.   75s.

12. 1769 **Elizabeth Montagu**
An Essay on the Writings and Genius of Shakespear, compared with the Greek and French dramatic Poets. With some
remarks upon the misrepresentations of Mons. de Voltaire
(1769)
iv, 288p.   90s.

13. 1774 **William Richardson**
     1784 Essays on Shakespeare's Dramatic Characters: With an
     1789 Illustration of Shakespeare's Representation of National
           Character, in that of Fluellen (sixth edition 1812)
           xii, 448p.   £6 6s.

14. 1775 **Elizabeth Griffith**
The Morality of Shakespeare's Drama Illustrated (1775)
xvi, 528p.   £9 9s.

15. 1777 **Maurice Morgann**
An Essay on the Dramatic Character of Sir John Falstaff
(1777)
xii, 186p.   63s.

16. 1783 **Joseph Ritson**
Remarks Critical and Illustrative of the last Edition of
Shakespeare [by George Steevens, 1778], (1783)
viii, 240p.
     1788 **Joseph Ritson**
The Quip Modest; A few Words by way of Supplement to
Remarks, Critical and Illustrative on the Text and Notes of
the Last Edition of Shakespeare: occasioned by a Republi-
cation of that Edition (1788, first issue)
viii, 32p.
With the preface (revised) to the second issue of *The Quip
Modest* (1788)
viii p.   84s.

17. 1785 **Thomas Whately**
Remarks on some of the Characters of Shakespere, Edited

by Richard Whately (Third edition 1839)
128p.   55s.

18. 1785   **John Monck Mason**
    1797   Comments on the Several Editions of Shakespeare's Plays,
    1798   Extended to those of Malone and Steevens (1807)
           xvi, 608p.   £9 9s.

19. 1786   **John Philip Kemble**
           Macbeth and King Richard the Third: An Essay, in answer to
           Remarks on some of the Characters of Shakespeare [by
           Thomas Whately] (1817)
           xii, 172p.   63s.

20. 1792   **Joseph Ritson**
           Cursory Criticisms on the Edition of Shakespeare published
           by Edmond Malone (1792)
           x, 104p.
           Edmond Malone
           A Letter to the Rev. Richard Farmer, D.D. Master of
           Emanuel College, Cambridge; Relative to the Edition of
           Shakespeare, published in 1790. And Some Late Criticisms
           on that work (1792)
           ii, 40p.   60s.

21. 1796   **William Henry Ireland**
           An Authentic Account of the Shakespeare Manuscripts (1796)
           ii, 44p.
    1799   **William Henry Ireland**
           Vortigern, An Historical Tragedy, In five Acts; Represented
           at the Theatre Royal, Drury Lane. And Henry the Second,
           An Historical Drama. Supposed to be written by the Author
           of Vortigern (1799)
           8o, iv, 79p.   75s.

22. 1796   **Edmond Malone**
           An Inquiry into the Authenticity of Certain Miscellaneous
           Papers and Legal Instruments, published Dec. 24, 1795. And
           Attributed to Shakespeare, Queen Elizabeth, and Henry
           Earl of Southampton (1796)
           vii, 424p.   £7

23. 1796 **Thomas Caldecott**
Mr. Ireland's Vindication of his Conduct, Respecting the
Publication of the Supposed Shakespeare Manuscripts (1796)
iv, 48p.

    1800 **George Hardinge**
Chalmeriana: or a Collection of Papers . . . occasioned by
reading a late Apology for the Believers in the Shakespeare
papers, by George Chalmers etc. (1800)
viii, 94p.   60s.

24. 1798 **Samuel Ireland**
An Investigation of Mr. Malone's Claim to the Character of
Scholar, or Critic, Being an Examination of his Inquiry into
the Authenticity of the Shakespeare Manuscripts, etc. (1797)
vi, 156p.   63s.

25. 1797 **George Chalmers**
An Apology for the Believers in the Shakespeare-Papers
which were exhibited in Norfolk Street (1797)
iv, 628p.   £9 9s.

26. 1799 **George Chalmers**
A Supplemental Apology for the Believers in the Shakespeare-
Papers: Being a Reply to Mr. Malone's Answer, which was
early announced, but never published: with a Dedication to
George Steevens, and a Postscript (1799)
viii, 656 p.   £9 9s.

Date Due

CAT. NO. 23 233   PRINTED IN U.S.A.